SCAN & SING

VOLUMES 1 & 2

How To Use This Book

Thank you for purchasing Scan & Sing Volumes 1&2! This book includes QR codes for 1,000+ (1,008 to be exact) compiled popular karaoke songs from the first two volumes. But that's not all - we've added a Table of Contents to make it even easier to find the songs you want to sing. With the ability to search alphabetically by song title and artist, you'll be able to quickly and easily find the perfect song for any occasion.

If you like to Scan & Sing, leave us an Amazon review or email us at dreamingtreepublishing@gmail.com!

1. Choose a Song

Use the Table of Contents to find a song you'd like to perform. Songs are organized alphabetically by artist.

2. Scan a Song With Your Phone

Use your smartphone's camera or a QR code/barcode reader application to scan and launch a song's associated karaoke video.

3. Screenshare or Cast to Your TV

Using Chromecast or other screensharing software, cast your chosen video to your screen, and get ready to perform!

Alphabetical By Artist

Song	Page
*NSYNC - Tearin' Up My Heart	1
*NSYNC - This I Promise You	1
*NSYNC - It's Gonna Be Me	1
*NSYNC - Bye Bye Bye	1
*NSYNC - God Must Have Spent A Little More Time On You	1
21 Savage - Bank Account	1
3 Doors Down - Here Without You	1
3 Doors Down - Kryptonite	1
3 Doors Down - When I'm Gone	1
4 Non Blondes - What's Up	2
a-ha - Take On Me	2
ABBA - Dancing Queen	2
ABBA - Mama Mia	2
ABBA - Chiquitita	2
ABBA - Fernando	2
ABBA - Take a Chance on Me	2
AC/DC - Dirty Deeds Done Dirt Cheap	2
Adele - Make You Feel My Love	2
Adele - Someone Like You	3
Adele - Set Fire To The Rain	3
Adele - When We Were Young	3
Adele - Turning Tables	3
Adele - Hello	3
Adele - Easy On Me	3
Adele - Rolling in the Deep	3
Adele - Rumor Has It	3
Aerosmith - I Don't Wanna Miss A Thing	3
Aerosmith - Jaded	4
Aerosmith - Walk This Way	4
Aerosmith - Cryin'	4
Aerosmith - Dream On	4
Air Supply - All Out of Love	4
Air Supply - Chances	4
Aladdin - Prince Ali	4
Aladdin - A Whole New World	4
Alan Walker - Faded	4
Alanis Morisette - Ironic	5
Alanis Morisette - You Oughta Know	5
Alanis Morisette - Hand In My Pocket	5
Alanis Morisette - Head Over Feet	5
Alanis Morisette - Uninvited	5
Alessia Cara - How Far I'll Go	5
Alex & Sierra - Little Do You Know	5
Alex Clare - Too Close	5
Alicia Keys - Girl On Fire	5
Alicia Keys - If I Ain't Got You	6
Alicia Keys - No One	6
Alicia Keys - Fallin'	6
Alicia Keys - Unthinkable (I'm Ready)	6
America - A Horse With No Name	6
America - Sister Golden Hair	6

Amy Winehouse - Rehab 6
Amy Winehouse - Back to Black 6
Amy Winehouse - You Know I'm No Good 6
Amy Winehouse & Mark Ronson - Valerie 7
Anne Murray - I Just Fall In Love Again 7
Aqua - Barbie Girl 7
Aretha Franklin - I Say a Little Prayer 7
Ariana Grande - Dangerous Woman 7
Ariana Grande - 7 Rings 7
Ariana Grande - One Last Time 7
Ariana Grande - Breathin' 7
Ariana Grande - Tattooed Heart 7
Ariana Grande, John Legend - Beauty & The Beast 8
Audioslave - Like a Stone 8
Audrey Hepburn - Moon River 8
Auli'i Cravalho - How Far I'll Go 8
Ava Max - Kings & Queens 8
Ava Max - Sweet But Psycho 8
Ava Max - So Am I 8
Avirl Lavigne - Complicated 8
Avirl Lavigne - I'm With You 8
Avirl Lavigne - Sk8er Boi 9
Avirl Lavigne - My Happy Ending 9
Avirl Lavigne - Girlfriend 9
Avirl Lavigne - When You're Gone 9
B-52's - Love Shack 9
B.J. Thomas - Raindrops Keep Falling on My Head 9
Backstreet Boys - I Want It That Way 9
Backstreet Boys - As Long As You Love Me 9
Backstreet Boys - Show Me The Meaning Of Being Lonely 9
Backstreet Boys - Everybody (Backstreet's Back) 10
Backstreet Boys - Shape Of My Heart 10
Backstreet Boys - All I Have To Give 10
Backstreet Boys - Quit Playing Games With My Heart 10
Bad Bunny - Yonaguni 10
Bad Bunny - Moscow Mule 10
Bad Bunny - Callaíta 10
Band of Horses - The Funeral 10
Band of Horses - No One's Gonna Love You 10
Barenaked Ladies - It's All Been Done 11
Barenaked Ladies - One Week 11
Barenaked Ladies - If I Had A Million Dollars 11
Barenaked Ladies - Alcohol 11
Beastie Boys - Fight For Your Right 11
Beastie Boys - No Sleep Till Brooklyn 11
Beatles - In My Life 11
Beauty And The Beast - Tale As Old As Time 11
Beauty And The Beast - Belle 11
Beauty And The Beast - Be Our Guest 12
Bee Gees - Stayin' Alive 12
Bee Gees - To Love Somebody 12
Ben E. King - Stand By Me 12
Ben Howard - Keep Your Head Up 12
Beyoncé - Single Ladies 12
Beyoncé - Pretty Hurts 12
Beyoncé - Cuff It 12
Beyoncé - I Was Here 12
Beyoncé - Break My Soul 13

Beyoncé - Halo 13
Beyoncé - Listen 13
Beyoncé - Single Ladies 13
Beyoncé - Love On Top 13
Beyoncé - If I Were A Boy 13
Beyoncé - Irreplaceable 13
Beyoncé ft Jay-Z - Drunk In Love 13
Beyoncé ft Jay-Z - Hey 13
Big & Rich - Save A Horse Ride A Cowboy 14
Big Star - Thirteen 14
Bill Medley, Jennifer Warnes - (I've Had) The Time Of My Life 14
Billie Eilish - idontwanttobeyouanymore 14
Billie Eilish - lovely 14
Billie Eilish - lovely (with Khalid) 14
Billie Eilish - i love you 14
Birdy - Skinny Love 14
Billy Joel - Just The Way You Are 14
Billy Joel - Piano Man 15
Billy Joel - Uptown Girl 15
Blondie - Heart of Glass 15
Blondie - One Way Or Another 15
Blue Öyster Cult - Don't Fear the Reaper 15
Blue Swede, Bjorn Skifs - Hooked on a Feeling 15
Bo Burnham - All Eyes On Me 15
Bo Burnham - Comedy 15
Bo Burnham - Goodbye (Possible Ending Song) 15
Bo Burnham - That Funny Feeling 16
Bo Burnham - Welcome To The Internet 16
Bo Burnham - Bezos 1 16
Bo Burnham - Bezos 2 16
Bo Burnham - Content 16
Bo Burnham - White Woman's Instagram 16
Bo Burnham - "1985" 16
Bob Dylan - Like a Rolling Stone 16
Bob Dylan - Hey, Mr. Tambourine Man 16
Bob Dylan - The Times, They Are A-Changin' 17
Bob Dylan - Knockin' On Heaven's Door 17
Bob Seger - Turn The Page 17
Bob Seger - Against The Wind 17
Bob Seger - Night Moves 17
Bob Seger - Old TIme Rock & Roll 17
Bob Seger - Like a Rock 17
Bon Jovi - Livin' On A Prayer 17
Bon Jovi - Always 17
Bon Jovi - Thank You For Loving Me 18
Bon Jovi - It's My Life 18
Bon Jovi - Wanted Dead Or Alive 18
Bon Jovi - You Give Love a Bad Name 18
Bon Jovi - Livin' On A Prayer 18
Bonnie Tyler - Total Eclipse Of The Heart 18
Boston - More Than a Feeling 18
Brian McKnight - One Last Cry 18
Brian McKnight - Back At One 18
Bright Eyes - The First Day Of My Life 19
Britney Spears - Oops!... I Did it Again 19
Britney Spears - ...Baby One More Time 19
Britney Spears - Toxic 19
Britney Spears - Sometimes 19

Britney Spears - Everytime 19

Britney Spears - Lucky 19

Britney Spears - Womanizer 19

Britney Spears - Stronger 19

Bruno Mars - When I Was Your Man 20

Bruno Mars - Leave The Door Open 20

Bruno Mars - Locked Out Of Heaven 20

Bruno Mars - Grenade 20

Bruno Mars - The Lazy Song 20

Bruno Mars - Just The Way You Are 20

Bruno Mars - Marry You 20

Bruno Mars - Talking To The Moon 20

Bruno Mars & Mark Ronson - Uptown Funk 20

Bryan Adams - Everything I Do (I Do It For You) 21

Bryan Adams - Please Forgive Me 21

BTS - Dynamite 21

BTS - Permission to Dance 21

BTS - Butter 21

BTS - Life Goes On 21

Buddy Holly - That'll Be The Day 21

Bush - Glycerine 21

Calum Scott - You Are The Reason 21

Camila Cabello ft. Young Thug - Havana 22

Carl Douglas - Kung Fu Fighting 22

Carly Rae Jepsen - Call Me Maybe 22

Carly Simon - You're So Vain 22

Carpenters - We've Only Just Begun 22

Carpenters - I Won't Last A Day Without You 22

Carrie Underwood - Before He Cheats 22

Cascada - Every Time We Touch 22

Celine Dion - My Heart Will Go On 22

Celine Dion - It's All Coming Back To Me Now 23

Chainsmoker ft. Kelsea Ballerini - This Feeling 23

Chainsmokers - Paris 23

Chainsmokers ft. Coldplay - Somthing Just Like This 23

Chainsmokers ft. Daya - Don't Let Me Down 23

Chainsmokers ft. Halsey - Closer 23

Chainsmokers ft. Lennon Stella - Illenium 23

Chainsmokers ft. Phoebe Ryan - All We Know 23

Chainsmokers ft. Rozes - Roses 23

Charlie Puth - One Call Away 24

Charlie Puth - Attention 24

Charlie Puth - How Long 24

Charlie Puth - That's Hilarious 24

Charlie Puth - Light Switch 24

Charlie Puth - The Way I Am 24

Cher - You Haven't Seen The Last Of Me 24

Chris DeBurgh - Lady In Red 24

Chris Stapleton - Tennessee Whiskey 24

Christina Aguilera - Hurt 25

Christina Aguilera - Genie In A Bottle 25

Christina Aguilera - Beautiful 25

Christina Perri - A Thousand Years 25

Christina Perri - Jar Of Hearts 25

Chubby Checker - Let's Twist Again 25

Chuck Berry - Johnny B. Goode 25

Chuck Berry - You Never Can Tell 25

Chumbawamba - Tubthumping 25

Colbie Caillat - Bubbly 26
Coldplay - Fix You 26
Coldplay - The Scientist 26
Coldplay - Yellow 26
Coldplay - Viva La Vida 26
Coldplay - Don't Panic 26
Commodores - Easy 26
Counting Crows - Mr. Jones 26
Creed - My Sacrifice 26
Creed - Higher 27
Creed - One Last Breath 27
Creed - With Arms Wide Open 27
Creedence Clearwater Revival - Lookin' Out My Back Door 27
Creedence Clearwater Revival - Have You Ever Seen the Rain 27
Creedence Clearwater Revival - Proud Mary 27
Creedence Clearwater Revival - Bad Moon Rising 27
Creedence Clearwater Revival - I Heard It Through The Grapevine 27
Creedence Clearwater Revival - Fortunate Son 27
Creedence Clearwater Revival - Jambalaya 28
Crowded House - Don't Dream It's Over 28
Cults - Always Forever 28
Cyndi Lauper - Girls Just Want To Have Fun 28
Daniel Powter - Bad Day 28
David Bowie - Ziggy Stardust 28
David Guetta ft. Sia - Titanium 28
Dean Martin - Sway 28
Death Cab For Cutie - I Will Follow You Into The Dark 28
Del Shannon - Runaway 29
Demi Lovato - Heart Attack 29
Demi Lovato - Stone Cold 29
Demi Lovato - La La Land 29
Demi Lovato - Skyscraper 29
Demi Lovato - Don't Forget 29
Demi Lovato - Warrior 29
Demi Lovato - Give Your Heart a Break 29
Demi Lovato - Anyone 29
Demi Lovato - Wihtout the Love 30
Demi Lovato - Neon Lights 30
Depeche Mode - Personal Jesus 30
Depeche Mode - Enjoy the Silence 30
Destiny's Child - Bootylicious 30
Destiny's Child - Say My Name 30
Destiny's Child - Emotion 30
Dexy's Midnight Runners - Come on Eileen 30
Dion - The Wanderer 30
Dion & The Belmonts - Teenager in Love 31
Dixie Chicks - Wide Open Spaces 31
DNCE - Cake by the Ocean 31
Doja Cat - Streets 31
Doja Cat - Say So 31
Doja Cat - Woman 31
Doja Cat ft. SZA - Kiss Me More 31
Doja Cat, The Weeknd - You Right 31
Dolly Parton - Jolene 31
Dolly Parton - 9 To 5 32
Don McLean - Vincent 32
Don McLean - American Pie 32
Donna Lewis - I Love You Always Forever 32

Donna Summer - Last Dance 32
Donna Summer - Hot Stuff 32
Donovan - Season of the Witch 32
Dua Lipa - Levitating 32
Dua Lipa - IDGAF 32
Dua Lipa - New Rules 33
Dua Lipa - Don't Start Now 33
Dua Lipa - Love Again 33
Dua Lipa - Break My Heart 33
Dusty Springfield - You Don't Have To Say You Love Me 33
Eagles - Take It Easy 33
Eagles - Hotel California 33
Earth, Wind and Fire - September 33
Ed Sheeran - Perfect 33
Ed Sheeran - Shape of You 34
Ed Sheeran - Thinking Out Loud 34
Ed Sheeran - Photograph 34
Ed Sheeran - Bad Habits 34
Edward Sharpe & The Magnetic Zeros - Home 34
Eiffel 65 - Blue 34
Electric Light Orchestra - Mr. Blue Sky 34
Electric Light Orchestra - Don't Bring Me Down 34
Electric Light Orchestra - Livin' Thing 34
Ellie Goulding - Love Me Like You Do 35
Ellie Goulding - Burn 35
Ellie Goulding - Lights 35
Ellie Goulding - Still Falling For You 35
Ellie Goulding - On My Mind 35
Ellie Goulding - Army 35
Elliot Smith - Between the Bars 35
Elliot Smith - Angeles 35
Elliot Smith - Somebody That I Used To Know 35
Elliot Smith - A Fond Farewell 36
Elliot Smith - Waltz #2 36
Elliot Smith - Son of Sam 36
Elliot Smith - Everything Reminds Me of Her 36
Elton John - Your Song 36
Elton John - Tiny Dancer 36
Elton John - Don't Let The Sun Go Down On Me 36
Elton John - I Guess That's Why They Call It The Blues 36
Elton John - Bennie And The Jets 36
Elton John - Don't Go Breaking My Heart 37
Elton John - Rocket Man 37
Elton John - Crocodile Rock 37
Elvis Presley - It's Now Or Never 37
Elvis Presley - Can't Help Falling In Love 37
Elvis Presley - If I Can Dream 37
Elvis Presley - Jailhouse Rock 37
Elvis Presley - Hound Dog 37
Elvis Presley - Suspicious Minds 37
Elvis Presley - Don't Be Cruel 38
Elvis Presley - That's All Right 38
Elvis Presley - It's Now Or Never 38
Elvis Presley - Always On My Mind 38
Eminem - Lose Yourself 38
Eminem - Without Me 38
Eminem - The Real Slim Shady 38
Eminem - Mockingbird 38

Eminem & Rihanna - Love The Way You Lie 38
Eminem ft Dido - Stan 39
Encanto - We Don't Talk About Bruno 39
Enrique Iglesias - Hero 39
Eric Clapton - Tears in Heaven 39
Eric Clapton - Wonderful Tonight 39
Eurythmics - Sweet Dreams 39
Everly Brothers - Crying In The Rain 39
Faith Hill - This Kiss 39
Fifth Harmony - Worth It 39
Fifth Harmony - I'm in Love with a Monster 40
Fifth Harmony - Miss Movin' On 40
Fifth Harmony - Bo$$ 40
Fifth Harmony ft. Ty Dolla Sign - Work From Home 40
Fleet Foxes - Mykonos 40
Fleetwood Mac - Landslide 40
Flo Rida - Whistle 40
Flo Rida - My House 40
Flo Rida - Good Feeling 40
Flo Rida, David Guetta - Club Can't Handle Me 41
Flo Rida, Ke$ha - Right Round 41
Flo Rida, T-Pain - Low 41
Foreigner - I Want To Know What Love Is 41
Frank Sinatra - Strangers In The Night 41
Frank Sinatra - New York, New York 41
Frank Sinatra - The Way You Look Tonight 41
Frank Sinatra - Fly Me To The Moon 41
Frank Sinatra - My Way 41
Frank Sinatra - Come Fly With Me 42
Frankie Valli and the Four Seasons - I Can't Take My Eyes Off You 42
Frankie Valli and the Four Seasons - Sherry 42
Frankie Valli and the Four Seasons - Bye Bye Baby (Baby Goodbye) 42
Frankie Valli and the Four Seasons - Walk Like a Man 42
Franz Ferdinand - Take Me Out 42
Frou Frou - Let Go 42
Frozen - Let It Go 42
Frozen - For The First Time In Forever 42
Frozen - Love Is An Open Door 43
Frozen 2 - Into the Unknown 43
Frozen 2 - All is Found 43
Fun - Some Nights 43
Garbage - Only Happy When It Rains 43
Gary Jules - Mad World 43
GAYLE - abcdefu 43
Gazebo - I Like Chopin 43
George Ezra - Budapest 43
George Michael - Faith 44
Gloria Gaynor - I Will Survive 44
Gnarls Barkely - Crazy 44
Goo Goo Dolls - Iris 44
Gordon Lightfoot - Wreck of the Edmund Fitzgerald 44
Gorillaz - Feel Good, Inc 44
Gorillaz - Clint Eastwood 44
Gotye and Kimbra - Somebody That I Used To Know 44
Grace VanderWaal - I Don't Know My Name 44
Grease - There Are Worse Things I Could Do 45
Grease - You're The One That I Want 45
Grease - Hopelessly Devoted To You 45

Grease - Summer Nights 45
Green Day - Good Riddance (Time of Your Life) 45
Green Day - Too Dumb to Die 45
Grizzly Bear - Two Weeks 45
Guns N' Roses - Patience 45
Guns N' Roses - Don't Cry 45
Guns N' Roses - November Rain 46
Guns N' Roses - Welcome to the Jungle 46
Guns N' Roses - Sweet Child of Mine 46
Hall & Oates - Maneater 46
Hall/Oates - You Make My Dreams Come True 46
Halsey - Without Me 46
Halsey - Bad at Love 46
Halsey - You Should Be Sad 46
Halsey - Colors 46
Halsey - Gasoline 47
Halsey - So Good 47
Halsey - Castle 47
Halsey - Eyes Closed 47
Hank Williams, Jr. - Your Cheatin' Heart 47
Hanson - MMMBop 47
Harry Chapin - Cat's In The Cradle 47
Harry Chapin - I Wanna Learn a Love Song 47
Harry Chapin - Better Place To Be 47
Harry Chapin - Taxi 48
Harry Styles - Sign Of The Times 48
Harry Styles - Falling 48
Harry Styles - As It Was 48
Harry Stylez - Sweet Creatures 48
Harry Stylez - Kiwi 48
Harry Stylez - Watermelon Sugar 48
Harry Stylez - Adore You 48
Harry Stylez - Matilda 48
Harry Stylez - Boyfriends 49
Harvey Danger - Flagpole Sitta 49
Heart - These Dreams 49
Hercules - Go the Distance 49
Herman's Hermits - There's a Kind of Hush 49
House Of Pain - Jump Around 49
Hozier - Take Me To Church 49
Imagine Dragons - Demons 49
Imagine Dragons - Believer 49
Imagine Dragons - Sharks 50
Imagine Dragons - Thunder 50
Imagine Dragons - Radioactive 50
Ingrid Michaelson - The Way I Am 50
Ingrid Michaelson - You And I 50
Israel Kamakawiwo'ole - Over The Rainbow / What a Wonderful World 50
James Blunt - You're Beautiful 50
James Brown - I Got You (I Feel Good) 50
James Brown - Papa's Got A Brand New Bag 50
James Brown - It's a Man's Man's Man's World 51
James Brown - Get Up Offa That Thing 51
James Taylor - Fire and Rain 51
James Taylor - Sweet Baby James 51
Jason Mraz, Colbie Caillat - Lucky 51
Jax - I Know Victoria's Secret 51
Jeff Buckley - Hallelujah 51

Jessie J - Flashlight 51
Jessie J - Who You Are 51
Jessie J - Masterpiece 52
Jessie J - Domino 52
Jessie J ft. B.o.B - Price Tag 52
Jessie J, Ariana Grande, Nicki Minaj - Bang Bang 52
Jewel - Foolish Games 52
Jim Croce - Bad Bad Leroy Brown 52
Jim Croce - I Got a Name 52
Jim Croce - Time In A Bottle 52
Jim Croce - I'll Have To Say I Love You In A Song 52
Jimi Hendrix - All Along the Watchtower 53
Jimi Hendrix - Purple Haze 53
Jimi Hendrix - Voodoo Child 53
Jimmy Cliff - I Can See Clearly Now 53
Joan Jett - I Love Rock 'N Roll 53
Joe Cocker - With A Little Help From My Friends 53
John Denver - Take Me Home, Country Roads 53
John Denver - Leaving On a Jet Plane 53
John Denver - Thank God I'm a Country Boy 53
John Legend - All Of Me 54
John Lennon - Imagine 54
John Lennon - Jealous Guy 54
John Mellencamp - Hurts So Good 54
Johnny Cash - Ring of Fire 54
Johnny Cash - I Walk the Line 54
Johnny Cash - Hurt 54
Joji - Test Drive 54
Joji - Glimpse of Us 54
Joji - Sanctuary 55
Jonas Brothers - Only Human 55
Jonas Brothers - Sucker 55
Journey - Don't Stop Believin' 55
Judy Garland - Somewhere Over the Rainbow 55
Juice WRLD - Lucid Dreams 55
Justin Bieber - Baby 55
Justin Bieber - Sorry 55
Justin Bieber - Love Yourself 55
Justin Bieber - Boyfriend 56
Justin Timberlake - Can't Stop The Feeling 56
Justin Timberlake - Mirrors 56
JVKE - Upside Down 56
JVKE - This is What Heartbreak Feels Like 56
JVKE - Golden Hour 56
JVKE - This is What Falling in Love Feels Like 56
Kansas - Dust In The Wind 56
Kate Bush - Running Up That Hill 56
Katrina And The Waves - Walking On Sunshine 57
Katy Perry - Roar 57
Katy Perry - Hot 'n' Cold 57
Katy Perry - Firework 57
Katy Perry - Last Friday Night (T.G.I.F.) 57
Katy Perry - E.T. 57
Katy Perry - The One That Got Away 57
Katy Perry - I Kissed a Girl 57
Katy Perry - Dark Horse 57
KC And The Sunshine Band - That's The Way (I Like It) ... 58
Ke$ha - TiK ToK 58

Ke$ha - Praying 58
Keane - Somewhere Only We Know 58
Keane - This Is The Last Time 58
Keane - Everybody's Changing 58
Keane - She Has No Time 58
Keane - Bedshaped 58
Keane - Bend and Break 58
Keane - We Might As Well Be Strangers 59
Kelly Clarkson - Since U Been Gone 59
Kelly Clarkson - Because Of You 59
Kelly Clarkson - Breakaway 59
Kelly Clarkson - A Moment Like This 59
Kelly Clarkson - Piece By Piece 59
KISS - I Was Made For Lovin' You 59
KISS - Rock and Roll All Nite 59
KT Tunstall - Suddenly I See 59
KT Tunstall - Black Horse and a Cherry Tree 60
Lady Gaga - Bad Romance 60
Lady Gaga - I'll Never Love Again 60
Lady Gaga - Million Reasons 60
Lady Gaga - Paparazzi 60
Lady Gaga - Born This Way 60
Lady Gaga - Always Remember Us This Way 60
Lady Gaga, Bradley Cooper - Shallow 60
Summertime Sadness - Lana Del Rey 60
Lauper - Girls Just Want to Have Fun 61
LeAnn Rimes - How Do I Live 61
LeAnn Rimes - Can't Fight The Moonlight 61
Led Zeppelin - Stairway To Heaven 61
Lee Ann Womack - I Hope You Dance 61
Lemon Tree - Fool's Garden 61
Leona Lewis - Bleeding Love 61
Letters to Cleo - Cruel to Be Kind 61
Lewis Capaldi - Someone You Loved 61
Lil Nas X - Montero (Call Me By Your Name) 62
Lil Nas X - Old Town Road 62
Lil Nas X - That's What I Want 62
Lil Nas X - Sun Goes Down 62
Lil Nas X - Panini 62
Lil Nas X ft Jack Harlow - Industry Baby 62
Lionel Richie - Hello 62
Lionel Richie - Stuck On You 62
Lionel Richie, Diana Ross - Endless Love 62
Little Richard - Tutti Frutti 63
Lizzo - Truth Hurts 63
Lizzo - Juice 63
Lizzo ft. Ariana Grande - Good As Hell 63
Lou Bega - Mambo No. 5 63
Louis Armstrong - What a Wonderful World 63
Lovin' Spoonful - What a Day for a Daydream 63
Lukas Graham - 7 Years 63
Luther Vandross - Dance With My Father 63
Lynrd Skynrd - Sweet Home Alabama 64
Lynrd Skynrd - Free Bird 64
Lynyrd Skynyrd - Simple Man 64
Macklemore & Ryan Lewis - Downtown 64
Macklemore & Ryan Lewis - Can't Hold Us 64
Macklemore & Ryan Lewis - Thrift Shop 64

Macklemore & Ryan Lewis - Same Love 64
Madonna - Material Girl 64
Madonna - Like A Prayer 64
Magic! - Rude 65
Manfred Mann - Blinded By The Light 65
Mariah Carey - Without You 65
Mariah Carey - Hero 65
Mariah Carey - Always Be My Baby 65
Mariah Carey - We Belong Together 65
Maroon 5 - Sunday Morning 65
Maroon 5 - This Love 65
Maroon 5 - Sugar 65
Maroon 5 - Beautiful Mistakes 66
Maroon 5 - She Will Be Loved 66
Marvin Gaye - Sexual Healing 66
Marvin Gaye, Tammi Terrell - Ain't No Mountain High Enough 66
Meghan Trainor - No 66
Meghan Trainor - Me Too 66
Meghan Trainor - Lips Are Movin' 66
Meghan Trainor - All About That Bass 66
Meghan Trainor - Made You Look 66
Meghan Trainor - Dear Future Husband 67
Meghan Trainor ft. John Legend - Like I'm Gonnea Lose You 67
Metallica - Nothing Else Matters 67
Michael Jackson - Billie Jean 67
Michael Jackson - Bad 67
Michael Jackson - Beat It 67
Michael Jackson - Smooth Criminal 67
Michael Jackson - Man in the Mirror 67
Michael Jackson - The Way You Make Me Feel 67
Michael Jackson - Thriller 68
Miley Cyrus - We Can't Stop 68
Miley Cyrus - When I Look At You 68
Miley Cyrus - Wrecking Ball 68
Miley Cyrus - The Climb 68
Miley Cyrus - Party In The USA 68
Mulan - Reflection 68
Mumford & Sons - I Will Wait 68
Mumford & Sons - Little Lion Man 68
Mumford and Sons - The Cave 69
Mumford and Sons - Awake My Soul 69
Muse - Starlight 69
My Chemical Romance - Welcome to the Black Parade 69
Naomi Scott - Speechless 69
Natalie Imbruglia - Torn 69
Natasha Bedingfield - Unwritten 69
Neil Diamond - Sweet Caroline 69
Nena - 99 Red Balloons 69
Niall Horan - Slow Hands 70
Niall Horan - This Town 70
Niall Horan - Too Much to Ask 70
Niall Horan - Flicker 70
Niall Horan - No Judgement 70
Nick Drake - One of These Things First 70
Nick Minaj - Super Bass 70
Nick Minaj - Anaconda 70
Nick Minaj - Chun-Li 70
Nick Minaj - Starships 71

Nick Minaj - Super Freaky Girl 71
Nickelback - How You Remind Me 71
Nickelback - Rockstar 71
Nickelback - Photograph 71
Nirvana - Heart-Shaped Box 71
Nirvana - Smells Like Teen Spirit 71
Nirvana - In Bloom 71
Nirvana - Come As You Are 71
Nitty Gritty Dirt Band - Mr. Bojangles 72
No Doubt - Don't Speak 72
Norman Greenbaum - Spirit in the Sky 72
Oasis - Champaign Supernova 72
Oasis - Wonderwall 72
Of Monsters And Men - Little Talks 72
Of Montreal - The Party's Crashing Us 72
OK Go - Get Over It 72
OK Go - Here It Goes Again 72
Olivia Rodrigo - deja vu 73
Olivia Rodrigo - drivers license 73
Olivia Rodrigo - happier 73
Olivia Rodrigo - All I Want 73
Olivia Rodrigo - favorite crime 73
Olivia Rodrigo - traitor 73
Olivia Rodrigo - good 4 u 73
Olivia Rodrigo - 1 step forward, 3 steps back 73
Olivia Rodrigo - jealousy, jealousy 73
Olivia Rodrigo - brutal 74
One Direction - Little Things 74
One Direction - Story Of My Life 74
One Direction - What Makes You Beautiful 74
One Direction - Kiss You 74
One Direction - Night Changes 74
One Direction - Best Song Ever 74
One Direction - More Than This 74
One Direction - Steal My Girl 74
One Direction - Love You Goodbye 75
One Direction - Infinity 75
OneRepublic - Counting Stars 75
OneRepublic - I Ain't Worried 75
Outkast - Hey Ya! 75
Owl City - Fireflies 75
P!nk - Raise Your Glass 75
P!nk - So What 75
P!nk - Try 75
P!nk - Sober 76
P!nk - Who Knew 76
P!nk - What About Us 76
Panic! at the Disco - I Write Sins Not Tragedies 76
Panic! at the Disco - Death of a Bachelor 76
Panic! at the Disco - The Ballad of Mona Lisa 76
Panic! at the Disco - Nine in the Afternoon 76
Panic! at the Disco - Girls/Girls/Boys 76
Panic! at the Disco - Always 76
Pat Benatar - Hit Me With Your Best Shot 77
Pat Benatar - We Belong 77
Pat Benatar - Love is a Battlefield 77
Paul Anka - Put Your Head On My Shoulder 77
Paul Anka - You Are My Destiny 77

Peaches & Herb - Shake Your Groove Thing 77
Petula Clark - Downtown 77
Pharrell Williams - Happy 77
Pharrell Williams - Freedom 77
Pink Floyd - Wish You Were Here 78
Pink Floyd - Shine On You Crazy Diamond 78
Pink Floyd - Comfortably Numb 78
Pink Floyd - Money 78
Pitbull and Ke$ha - Timber 78
Plain White T's - Hey There Delilah 78
Pocahontas - Colors Of The Wind 78
Pocahontas - Just Around The River Bend 78
Poison - Every Rose Has Its Thorn (With Lyrics) 78
Poison - Something To Believe In 79
Portugal the Man - Feel it Still 79
Post Malone - Circles 79
Post Malone, Swae Lee - Sunflower 79
Post Malone - I Like You 79
Prince - Kiss 79
Prince - Purple Rain 79
Queen - Another One Bites the Dust 79
Queen - Bohemian Rhapsody 79
Queen - Crazy Little Thing Called Love 80
Queen - Somebody To Love 80
Queen - Don't Stop Me Now 80
Queen - We Are The Champions 80
Queen - Love Of My Life 80
Queen - I Want To Break Free 80
R.E.M. - Losing My Religion 80
R.E.M. - Man on the Moon 80
R.E.M. - The One I Love 80
R.E.O. Speedwagon - Can't Fight This Feeling Anymore 81
Rachel Platten - Fight Song 81
Radiohead - Fake Plastic Trees 81
Radiohead - Creep 81
Ray Charles - Hit The Road Jack 81
Red Hot Chili Peppers - Under The Bridge 81
Red Hot Chili Peppers - Otherside 81
Red Hot Chili Peppers - Californication 81
Red Hot Chili Peppers - Scar Tissue 81
Redbone - Come and Get Your Love 82
Rent - Seasons of Love 82
Rick Springfield - Jessie's Girl 82
Right Said Fred - I'm Too Sexy 82
Rihanna - Diamonds 82
Rihanna - Love On The Brain 82
Rihanna, Mikky Ekko - Stay 82
Rolling Stones - Satisfaction 82
Rolling Stones - You Can't Always Get What You Want 82
Rolling Stones - Paint It Black 83
Rolling Stones - Beast of Burden 83
Roxette - Listen to Your Heart 83
Roy Orbison - Oh, Pretty Woman 83
Roy Orbison - Crying 83
Roy Orbison - You Got It 83
Roy Orbison - Only The Lonely 83
Rupert Holmes - Escape (The Pina Colada Song) 83
Ruth B - Lost Boy 83

Sam Smith - I'm Not the Only One 84
Sam Smith - Stay With Me 84
Sam Smith - Lay Me Down 84
Sam Smith - Too Good At Goodbyes 84
Sam Smith - Writing's On The Wall 84
Sam Smith - How Do You Sleep 84
Sam Smith - Like I Can 84
Sam Smith - Praying 84
Sara Bareilles - Love Song 84
Sara Bareilles - Gravity 85
Sara Bareilles - She Used to Be Mine 85
Sara Bareilles - I Choose You 85
Sara Bareilles - Brave 85
Sara McLachlan - Angel 85
Savage Garden - Truly Madly Deeply 85
Savage Garden - I Knew I Loved You 85
Seal - Kiss From a Rose 85
Selena - Dreaming of You 85
Selena Gomez - Same Old Love 86
Selena Gomez - Lose You To Love Me 86
Selena Gomez - Love You Like A Love Song 86
Selena Gomez - Slow Down 86
Selena Gomez - Hands to Myself 86
Selena Gomez - Kill Em With Kindness 86
Selena Gomez, Charlie Puth - We Don't Talk Anymore 86
Selena Gomez, Marshmello - Wolves 86
Selena Gomez, Rema - Calm Down 86
Selena Gomez, The Scene - A Year Without Rain 87
Shakira - Whenever, Wherever 87
Shakira - Hips Don't Lie 87
Shakira - Try Everything 87
Shakira - Underneath Your Clothes 87
Shania Twain - Walk The Moon 87
Shania Twain - Man! I Feel Like A Woman 87
Shania Twain - You're Still The One I Want 87
Shawn Mendes - Mercy 87
Shawn Mendes - Treat You Better 88
Shawn Mendes - Stitches 88
Shawn Mendes - There's Nothing Holding Me Back 88
Shawn Mendes, Camila Cabello - Senorita 88
Sia - Bird Set Free 88
Sia - Alive 88
Sia - Chandelier 88
Sia - Cheap Thrills 88
Sia - Snowman 88
Sia - Unstoppable 89
Sia - Elastic Heart 89
Sia - Fire Meet Gasoline 89
Simon & Garfunkel - Cecelia 89
Simon & Garfunkel - Mrs. Robinson 89
Simon & Garfunkel - Bridge Over Troubled Water 89
Simon & Garfunkel - The Sound Of Silence 89
Simon & Garfunkel - You Can Call Me Al 89
Simon & Garfunkel - The Only Living Boy In New York 89
Sinead O'Connor - Nothing Compares 2 U 90
Sir Mix-A-Lot - Baby Got Back 90
Sisqo - Incomplete 90
Sixpence None The Richer - Kiss Me 90

Smash Mouth - All Star 90
Soggy Bottom Boys - I Am A Man of Constant Sorrow 90
Sonny & Cher - I Got You Babe 90
Starland Vocal Band - Afternoon Delight 90
Starship - Nothing's Gonna Stop Us Now 90
Steve Lacy - Bad Habit 91
Steve Lacy - Dark Red 91
Steve Miller Band - The Joker 91
Stevie Wonder - I Just Called To Say I Love You 91
Stevie Wonder - Superstition 91
Stevie Wonder - My Cheri Amour 91
Stevie Wonder - Lately 91
Stevie Wonder - Signed, Sealed, Delivered I'm Yours 91
Sting - Shape of My Heart 91
Sting - Fields of Gold 92
Sting - Englishman in New York 92
Stone Temple Pilots - Plush 92
Stone Temple Pilots - Sour Girl 92
Stone Temple Pilots - Interstate Love Song 92
Stone Temple Pilots - Vaseline 92
Sufjan Stevens - Chicago 92
Sugar Ray - Every Morning 92
Sugar Ray - Fly 92
Supertramp - The Logical Song 93
Survivor - Eye Of The Tiger 93
Sweet Dreams (are made of this) - Eurythmics 93
System of a Down - Lonely Day 93
System of a Down - Toxicity 93
Tangerine Kitty - Dumb Ways To Die 93
Tarzan - You'll Be in My Heart 93
Taylor Swift - Blank Space 93
Taylor Swift - "22" 93
Taylor Swift - Love Story 94
Taylor Swift - You Belong With Me 94
Taylor Swift - I Knew You Were Trouble 94
Taylor Swift - Lover 94
Taylor Swift - Shake It Off 94
Taylor Swift - Look What You Made Me Do 94
Taylor Swift - We Are Never Ever Getting Back Together 94
Tenacious D - Kickapoo 94
Tenacious D - Tribute 94
The Angels - We Gotta Get Out of This Place 95
The Angels - My Boyfriend's Back 95
The Animals - Don't Let Me Be Misunderstood 95
The Archies - Sugar Sugar 95
The Beach Boys - Wouldn't It Be Nice 95
The Beach Boys - Help Me, Rhonda 95
The Beach Boys - Kokomo 95
The Beach Boys - Fun, Fun, Fun 95
The Beach Boys - California Girls 95
The Beach Boys - Don't Worry Baby 96
The Beach Boys - Surfin' USA 96
The Beach Boys - I Get Around 96
The Beach Boys - God Only Knows 96
The Beatles - Blackbird 96
The Beatles - Don't Let Me Down 96
The Beatles - Hey Jude 96
The Beatles - Here Comes The Sun 96

The Beatles - When I'm Sixty-Four 96
The Beatles - In My Life 97
The Beatles - I Saw Her Standing There 97
The Beatles - Yesterday 97
The Beatles - If I Fell 97
The Beatles - Ticket To Ride 97
The Beatles - I Want To Hold Your Hand 97
The Beatles - Let It Be 97
The Beatles - Ob-La-Di, Ob-La-Da 97
The Beatles - Come Together 97
The Beatles - And I Love Her 98
The Beatles - Eleanor Rigby 98
The Beatles - Till There Was You 98
The Beatles - With A Little Help From My Friends 98
The Beatles - Twist And Shout 98
The Beatles - The Long and Winding Road 98
The Cardigans - Lovefool 98
The Cascades - Rhythm of the Rain 98
The Clash - Should I Stay Or Should I Go 98
The Clash - I Fought The Law 99
The Cranberries - Dreams 99
The Cranberries - Zombie 99
The Divinyls - I Touch Myself 99
The Doors - Light My Fire 99
The Doors - Touch Me 99
The Doors - Riders on the Storm 99
The Doors - Break on Through 99
The Five Stairsteps - O-o-h Child 99
The Flaming Lips - Do You Realize 100
The Go-Go's - Vacation 100
The Go-Go's - Our Lips Are Sealed 100
The Go-Go's - We Got the Beat 100
The Jackson 5 - ABC 100
The Jackson 5 - I'll Be There 100
The Jackson 5 - I Want You Back 100
The Jonas Brothers - Burnin' Up 100
The Jonas Brothers - SOS 100
The Jonas Brothers - Lovebug 101
The Jonas Brothers - Year 3000 101
The Killers - Mr. Brightside 101
The Killers - All These Things That I've Done 101
The Killers - Somebody Told Me 101
The Killers - Smile Like You Mean It 101
The Killers - Human 101
The Killers - Jenny Was a Friend of Mine 101
The Kinks - You Really Got Me 101
The Lion King - Can You Feel The Love Tonight 102
The Lion King - I Just Can't Wait to Be King 102
The Lion King - Hakuna Matata 102
The Little Mermaid - Part of Your World 102
The Little Mermaid - Kiss The Girl 102
The Little Mermaid - Under The Sea 102
The Lovin' Spoonful - Do You Believe in Magic? 102
The Mamas and the Papas - Dream a Little Dream of Me 102
The Mommas and the Papas - California Dreamin' 102
The Monkees - I'm A Believer 103
The Monkees - Daydream Believer 103
The Overtones - Wake Me Up Before You Go Go 103

The Platters - Only You (And You Alone) 103
The Police - Roxanne 103
The Postal Service - Such Great Height 103
The Postal Service - The District Sleeps Alone Tonight 103
The Proclaimers - I'm Gonna Be (500 Miles) 103
The Ramones - I Wanna Be Sedated 103
The Ramones - Blitzkrieg Bop 104
The Righteous Brothers - Unchained Melody 104
The Rocky Horror Picture Show - Time Warp 104
The Rolling Stones - Gimme Shelter 104
The Ronettes - Be My Baby 104
The Shangri-Las - Leader of the Pack 104
The Shins - Caring is Creepy 104
The Shins - New Slang 104
The Smiths - There Is A Light That Never Goes Out 104
The Smiths - This Charming Man 105
The Smiths - Heaven Knows I'm Miserable Now 105
The Smiths - How Soon Is Now 105
The Verve - Bitter Sweet Symphony 105
The Wanted - Glad You Came 105
The Wanted - Chasing the Sun 105
The Wanted - We Own the Night 105
The Wanted - I Found You 105
The Weeknd - Blinding Lights 105
The Weeknd - Can't Feel My Face 106
The White Stripes - Seven Nation Army 106
The White Stripes - Fell In Love With a Girl 106
The White Stripes - The Hardest Button To Button 106
The Who - Behind Blue Eyes 106
The Who - Pinball Wizard 106
The Who - Baba O'Riley 106
The Wonders - That Thing You Do 106
Theme Song - Duck Tales 106
Theme Song - The Aadams Family 107
Theme Song - Friends (I'll Be There For You) 107
Theme Song - Pokemon 107
Theme Song - The Fresh Prince of Bel-Air 107
They Might Be Giants - Experimental Film 107
Thievery Corporation - Lebanese Blonde 107
Thin Lizzy - The Boys are Back in Town 107
Third Eye Blind - Semi-Charmed Life 107
Tim McGraw, Faith Hill - It's Your Love 107
Timbaland, One Republic - Apologize 108
Tina Turner - What's Love Got To Do With It 108
Tina Turner - The Best 108
TLC - Waterfalls 108
Tom Jones - You're My World 108
Tones & I - Dance Monkey 108
Tones & I - Fly Away 108
Toni Braxton - Unbreak My Heart 108
Toploader - Dancing In The Moonlight 108
Toto - Africa 109
Tracy Chapman - Fast Car 109
Train - Hey Soul Sister 109
Train - Drops of Jupiter 109
twenty one pilots - Stressed Out 109
twenty one pilots - Ride 109
twenty one pilots - House Of Gold 109

twenty one pilots - Chlorine 109
twenty one pilots - Car Radio 109
twenty one pilots - Migraine 110
twenty one pilots - Tear in My Heart 110
twenty one pilots - Heathens 110
U2 - With Or Without You 110
U2 - I Still Haven't Found What I'm Looking For 110
U2 - Sunday, Bloody Sunday 110
UB40 - Red Red Wine 110
Uncle Kracker & Dobie Gray - Drift Away 110
Usher, Alicia Keys - My Boo 110
Vance Joy - Riptide 111
Vanessa Carlton - A Thousand Miles 111
Vanilla Ice - Ice Ice Baby 111
Vertical Horizon - Everything You Want 111
Village People - YMCA 111
Weezer - Say it Ain't So 111
Weezer - Undone (The Sweater Song) 111
Weezer - Buddy Holly 111
Westlife - If I Let You Go 111
Wham! - Last Christmas 112
Whitney Houston - I Have Nothing 112
Whitney Houston - The Greatest Love Of All 112
Whitney Houston - Saving All My Love For You 112
Whitney Houston - I Wanna Dance With Somebody 112
Whitney Houston - I Will Always Love You 112
Wiz Khalifa ft. Charlie Puth - See You Again 112
XXXTENTACION - Changes 112
Zara Larsson - Uncover 112

Alphabetical By Title

Song	Page
...Baby One More Time - Britney Spears	19
"1985" - Bo Burnham	16
"22" - Taylor Swift	93
(I've Had) The Time Of My Life - Bill Medley, Jennifer Warnes	14
1 step forward, 3 steps back - Olivia Rodrigo	73
7 Rings - Ariana Grande	7
7 Years - Lukas Graham	63
9 To 5 - Dolly Parton	32
99 Red Balloons - Nena	69
A Fond Farewell - Elliot Smith	36
A Horse With No Name - America	6
A Moment Like This - Kelly Clarkson	59
A Thousand Miles - Vanessa Carlton	111
A Thousand Years - Christina Perri	25
A Whole New World - Aladdin	4
A Year Without Rain - Selena Gomez, The Scene	87
ABC - The Jackson 5	100
abcdefu - GAYLE	43
Adore You - Harry Stylez	48
Africa - Toto	109
Afternoon Delight - Starland Vocal Band	90
Against The Wind - Bob Seger	17
Ain't No Mountain High Enough - Marvin Gaye, Tammi Terrell	66
Alcohol - Barenaked Ladies	11
Alive - Sia	88
All About That Bass - Meghan Trainor	66
All Along the Watchtower - Jimi Hendrix	53
All Eyes On Me - Bo Burnham	15
All I Have To Give - Backstreet Boys	10
All I Want - Olivia Rodrigo	73
All is Found - Frozen 2	43
All Of Me - John Legend	54
All Out of Love - Air Supply	4
All Star - Smash Mouth	90
All These Things That I've Done - The Killers	101
All We Know - Chainsmokers ft. Phoebe Ryan	23
Always - Bon Jovi	17
Always - Panic! at the Disco	76
Always Be My Baby - Mariah Carey	65
Always Forever - Cults	28
Always On My Mind - Elvis Presley	38
Always Remember Us This Way - Lady Gaga	60
American Pie - Don McLean	32
Anaconda - Nick Minaj	70
And I Love Her - The Beatles	98
Angel - Sara McLachlan	85
Angeles - Elliot Smith	35
Another One Bites the Dust - Queen	79
Anyone - Demi Lovato	29
Apologize - Timbaland, One Republic	108
Army - Ellie Goulding	35

As It Was - Harry Styles 48
As Long As You Love Me - Backstreet Boys 9
Attention - Charlie Puth 24
Awake My Soul - Mumford and Sons 69
Baba O'Riley - The Who 106
Baby - Justin Bieber 55
Baby Got Back - Sir Mix-A-Lot 90
Back At One - Brian McKnight 18
Back to Black - Amy Winehouse 6
Bad - Michael Jackson 67
Bad at Love - Halsey 46
Bad Bad Leroy Brown - Jim Croce 52
Bad Day - Daniel Powter 28
Bad Habit - Steve Lacy 91
Bad Habits - Ed Sheeran 34
Bad Moon Rising - Creedence Clearwater Revival 27
Bad Romance - Lady Gaga 60
Bang Bang - Jessie J, Ariana Grande, Nicki Minaj 52
Bank Account - 21 Savage 1
Barbie Girl - Aqua 7
Be My Baby - The Ronettes 104
Be Our Guest - Beauty And The Beast 12
Beast of Burden - Rolling Stones 83
Beat It - Michael Jackson 67
Beautiful - Christina Aguilera 25
Beautiful Mistakes - Maroon 5 66
Beauty & The Beast - Ariana Grande, John Legend 8
Because Of You - Kelly Clarkson 59
Bedshaped - Keane 58
Before He Cheats - Carrie Underwood 22
Behind Blue Eyes - The Who 106
Believer - Imagine Dragons 49
Belle - Beauty And The Beast 11
Bend and Break - Keane 58
Bennie And The Jets - Elton John 36
Best Song Ever - One Direction 74
Better Place To Be - Harry Chapin 47
Between the Bars - Elliot Smith 35
Bezos 1 - Bo Burnham 16
Bezos 2 - Bo Burnham 16
Billie Jean - Michael Jackson 67
Bird Set Free - Sia 88
Bitter Sweet Symphony - The Verve 105
Black Horse and a Cherry Tree - KT Tunstall 60
Blackbird - The Beatles 96
Blank Space - Taylor Swift 93
Bleeding Love - Leona Lewis 61
Blinded By The Light - Manfred Mann 65
Blinding Lights - The Weeknd 105
Blitzkrieg Bop - The Ramones 104
Blue - Eiffel 65 34
Bo$$ - Fifth Harmony 40
Bohemian Rhapsody - Queen 79
Bootylicious - Destiny's Child 30
Born This Way - Lady Gaga 60
Boyfriend - Justin Bieber 56
Boyfriends - Harry Stylez 49

Brave - Sara Bareilles 85
Break My Heart - Dua Lipa 33
Break My Soul - Beyoncé 13
Break on Through - The Doors 99
Breakaway - Kelly Clarkson 59
Breathin' - Ariana Grande 7
Bridge Over Troubled Water - Simon & Garfunkel 89
brutal - Olivia Rodrigo 74
Bubbly - Colbie Caillat 26
Budapest - George Ezra 43
Buddy Holly - Weezer 111
Burn - Ellie Goulding 35
Burnin' Up - The Jonas Brothers 100
Butter - BTS 21
Bye Bye Baby (Baby Goodbye) - Frankie Valli and the Four Seasons 42
Bye Bye Bye - *NSYNC 1
Cake by the Ocean - DNCE 31
California Dreamin' - The Mommas and the Papas 102
California Girls - The Beach Boys 95
Californication - Red Hot Chili Peppers 81
Call Me Maybe - Carly Rae Jepsen 22
Callaíta - Bad Bunny 10
Calm Down - Selena Gomez, Rema 86
Can You Feel The Love Tonight - The Lion King 102
Can't Feel My Face - The Weeknd 106
Can't Fight The Moonlight - LeAnn Rimes 61
Can't Fight This Feeling Anymore - R.E.O. Speedwagon 81
Can't Help Falling In Love - Elvis Presley 37
Can't Hold Us - Macklemore & Ryan Lewis 64
Can't Stop The Feeling - Justin Timberlake 56
Car Radio - twenty one pilots 109
Caring is Creepy - The Shins 104
Castle - Halsey 47
Cat's In The Cradle - Harry Chapin 47
Cecelia - Simon & Garfunkel 89
Champaign Supernova - Oasis 72
Chances - Air Supply 4
Chandelier - Sia 88
Changes - XXXTENTACION 112
Chasing the Sun - The Wanted 105
Cheap Thrills - Sia 88
Chicago - Sufjan Stevens 92
Chiquitita - ABBA 2
Chlorine - twenty one pilots 109
Chun-Li - Nick Minaj 70
Circles - Post Malone 79
Clint Eastwood - Gorillaz 44
Closer - Chainsmokers ft. Halsey 23
Club Can't Handle Me - Flo Rida, David Guetta 41
Colors - Halsey 46
Colors Of The Wind - Pocahontas 78
Come and Get Your Love - Redbone 82
Come As You Are - Nirvana 71
Come Fly With Me - Frank Sinatra 42
Come on Eileen - Dexy's Midnight Runners 30
Come Together - The Beatles 97
Comedy - Bo Burnham 15

Comfortably Numb - Pink Floyd 78
Complicated - Avirl Lavigne 8
Content - Bo Burnham 16
Counting Stars - OneRepublic 75
Crazy - Gnarls Barkely 44
Crazy Little Thing Called Love - Queen 80
Creep - Radiohead 81
Crocodile Rock - Elton John 37
Cruel to Be Kind - Letters to Cleo 61
Cryin' - Aerosmith 4
Crying - Roy Orbison 83
Crying In The Rain - Everly Brothers 39
Cuff It - Beyoncé 12
Dance Monkey - Tones & I 108
Dance With My Father - Luther Vandross 63
Dancing In The Moonlight - Toploader 108
Dancing Queen - ABBA 2
Dangerous Woman - Ariana Grande 7
Dark Horse - Katy Perry 57
Dark Red - Steve Lacy 91
Daydream Believer - The Monkees 103
Dear Future Husband - Meghan Trainor 67
Death of a Bachelor - Panic! at the Disco 76
deja vu - Olivia Rodrigo 73
Demons - Imagine Dragons 49
Diamonds - Rihanna 82
Dirty Deeds Done Dirt Cheap - AC/DC 2
Do You Believe in Magic? - The Lovin' Spoonful 102
Do You Realize - The Flaming Lips 100
Domino - Jessie J 52
Don't Be Cruel - Elvis Presley 38
Don't Bring Me Down - Electric Light Orchestra 34
Don't Cry - Guns N' Roses 45
Don't Dream It's Over - Crowded House 28
Don't Fear the Reaper - Blue Öyster Cult 15
Don't Forget - Demi Lovato 29
Don't Go Breaking My Heart - Elton John 37
Don't Let Me Be Misunderstood - The Animals 95
Don't Let Me Down - Chainsmokers ft. Daya 23
Don't Let Me Down - The Beatles 96
Don't Let The Sun Go Down On Me - Elton John 36
Don't Panic - Coldplay 26
Don't Speak - No Doubt 72
Don't Start Now - Dua Lipa 33
Don't Stop Believin' - Journey 55
Don't Stop Me Now - Queen 80
Don't Worry Baby - The Beach Boys 96
Downtown - Macklemore & Ryan Lewis 64
Downtown - Petula Clark 77
Dream a Little Dream of Me - The Mamas and the Papas 102
Dream On - Aerosmith 4
Dreaming of You - Selena 85
Dreams - The Cranberries 99
Drift Away - Uncle Kracker & Dobie Gray 110
drivers license - Olivia Rodrigo 73
Drops of Jupiter - Train 109
Drunk In Love - Beyoncé ft Jay-Z 13

Duck Tales - Theme Song	106
Dumb Ways To Die - Tangerine Kitty	93
Dust In The Wind - Kansas	56
Dynamite - BTS	21
E.T. - Katy Perry	57
Easy - Commodores	26
Easy On Me - Adele	3
Elastic Heart - Sia	89
Eleanor Rigby - The Beatles	98
Emotion - Destiny's Child	30
Endless Love - Lionel Richie, Diana Ross	62
Englishman in New York - Sting	92
Enjoy the Silence - Depeche Mode	30
Escape (The Pina Colada Song) - Rupert Holmes	83
Eurythmics - Sweet Dreams (are made of this)	93
Every Morning - Sugar Ray	92
Every Rose Has Its Thorn (With Lyrics) - Poison	78
Every Time We Touch - Cascada	22
Everybody (Backstreet's Back) - Backstreet Boys	10
Everybody's Changing - Keane	58
Everything I Do (I Do It For You) - Bryan Adams	21
Everything Reminds Me of Her - Elliot Smith	36
Everything You Want - Vertical Horizon	111
Everytime - Britney Spears	19
Experimental Film - They Might Be Giants	107
Eye Of The Tiger - Survivor	93
Eyes Closed - Halsey	47
Faded - Alan Walker	4
Faith - George Michael	44
Fake Plastic Trees - Radiohead	81
Fallin' - Alicia Keys	6
Falling - Harry Styles	48
Fast Car - Tracy Chapman	109
favorite crime - Olivia Rodrigo	73
Feel Good, Inc - Gorillaz	44
Feel it Still - Portugal the Man	79
Fell In Love With a Girl - The White Stripes	106
Fernando - ABBA	2
Fields of Gold - Sting	92
Fight For Your Right - Beastie Boys	11
Fight Song - Rachel Platten	81
Fire and Rain - James Taylor	51
Fire Meet Gasoline - Sia	89
Fireflies - Owl City	75
Firework - Katy Perry	57
Fix You - Coldplay	26
Flagpole Sitta - Harvey Danger	49
Flashlight - Jessie J	51
Flicker - Niall Horan	70
Fly - Sugar Ray	92
Fly Away - Tones & I	108
Fly Me To The Moon - Frank Sinatra	41
Fool's Garden - Lemon Tree	61
Foolish Games - Jewel	52
For The First Time In Forever - Frozen	42
Fortunate Son - Creedence Clearwater Revival	27
Free Bird - Lynrd Skynrd	64

Freedom - Pharrell Williams	77
Friends (I'll Be There For You) - Theme Song	107
Fun, Fun, Fun - The Beach Boys	95
Gasoline - Halsey	47
Genie In A Bottle - Christina Aguilera	25
Get Over It - OK Go	72
Get Up Offa That Thing - James Brown	51
Gimme Shelter - The Rolling Stones	104
Girl On Fire - Alicia Keys	5
Girlfriend - Avirl Lavigne	9
Girls Just Want to Have Fun - Lauper	61
Girls Just Want To Have Fun - Cyndi Lauper	28
Girls/Girls/Boys - Panic! at the Disco	76
Give Your Heart a Break - Demi Lovato	29
Glad You Came - The Wanted	105
Glimpse of Us - Joji	54
Glycerine - Bush	21
Go the Distance - Hercules	49
God Must Have Spent A Little More Time On You - *NSYNC	1
God Only Knows - The Beach Boys	96
Golden Hour - JVKE	56
good 4 u - Olivia Rodrigo	73
Good As Hell - Lizzo ft. Ariana Grande	63
Good Feeling - Flo Rida	40
Good Riddance (Time of Your Life) - Green Day	45
Goodbye (Possible Ending Song) - Bo Burnham	15
Gravity - Sara Bareilles	85
Grenade - Bruno Mars	20
Hakuna Matata - The Lion King	102
Hallelujah - Jeff Buckley	51
Halo - Beyoncé	13
Hand In My Pocket - Alanis Morisette	5
Hands to Myself - Selena Gomez	86
happier - Olivia Rodrigo	73
Happy - Pharrell Williams	77
Havana - Camila Cabello ft. Young Thug	22
Have You Ever Seen the Rain - Creedence Clearwater Revival	27
Head Over Feet - Alanis Morisette	5
Heart Attack - Demi Lovato	29
Heart of Glass - Blondie	15
Heart-Shaped Box - Nirvana	71
Heathens - twenty one pilots	110
Heaven Knows I'm Miserable Now - The Smiths	105
Hello - Adele	3
Hello - Lionel Richie	62
Help Me, Rhonda - The Beach Boys	95
Here Comes The Sun - The Beatles	96
Here It Goes Again - OK Go	72
Here Without You - 3 Doors Down	1
Hero - Enrique Iglesias	39
Hero - Mariah Carey	65
Hey - Beyoncé ft Jay-Z	13
Hey Jude - The Beatles	96
Hey Soul Sister - Train	109
Hey There Delilah - Plain White T's	78
Hey Ya! - Outkast	75
Hey, Mr. Tambourine Man - Bob Dylan	16

Higher - Creed 27
Hips Don't Lie - Shakira 87
Hit Me With Your Best Shot - Pat Benatar 77
Hit The Road Jack - Ray Charles 81
Home - Edward Sharpe & The Magnetic Zeros 34
Hooked on a Feeling - Blue Swede, Bjorn Skifs 15
Hopelessly Devoted To You - Grease 45
Hot 'n' Cold - Katy Perry 57
Hot Stuff - Donna Summer 32
Hotel California - Eagles 33
Hound Dog - Elvis Presley 37
House Of Gold - twenty one pilots 109
How Do I Live - LeAnn Rimes 61
How Do You Sleep - Sam Smith 84
How Far I'll Go - Alessia Cara 5
How Far I'll Go - Auli'i Cravalho 8
How Long - Charlie Puth 24
How Soon Is Now - The Smiths 105
How You Remind Me - Nickelback 71
Human - The Killers 101
Hurt - Christina Aguilera 25
Hurt - Johnny Cash 54
Hurts So Good - John Mellencamp 54
I Ain't Worried - OneRepublic 75
I Am A Man of Constant Sorrow - Soggy Bottom Boys .. 90
I Can See Clearly Now - Jimmy Cliff 53
I Can't Take My Eyes Off You - Frankie Valli and the Four Seasons .. 42
I Choose You - Sara Bareilles 85
I Don't Know My Name - Grace VanderWaal 44
I Don't Wanna Miss A Thing - Aerosmith 3
I Fought The Law - The Clash 99
I Found You - The Wanted 105
I Get Around - The Beach Boys 96
I Got a Name - Jim Croce 52
I Got You (I Feel Good) - James Brown 50
I Got You Babe - Sonny & Cher 90
I Guess That's Why They Call It The Blues - Elton John .. 36
I Have Nothing - Whitney Houston 112
I Heard It Through The Grapevine - Creedence Clearwater Revival .. 27
I Hope You Dance - Lee Ann Womack 61
I Just Called To Say I Love You - Stevie Wonder 91
I Just Can't Wait to Be King - The Lion King 102
I Just Fall In Love Again - Anne Murray 7
I Kissed a Girl - Katy Perry 57
I Knew I Loved You - Savage Garden 85
I Knew You Were Trouble - Taylor Swift 94
I Know Victoria's Secret - Jax 51
I Like Chopin - Gazebo 43
I Like You - Post Malone 79
I Love Rock 'N Roll - Joan Jett 53
i love you - Billie Eilish 14
I Love You Always Forever - Donna Lewis 32
I Saw Her Standing There - The Beatles 97
I Say a Little Prayer - Aretha Franklin 7
I Still Haven't Found What I'm Looking For - U2 110
I Touch Myself - The Divinyls 99
I Walk the Line - Johnny Cash 54

I Wanna Be Sedated - The Ramones 103

I Wanna Dance With Somebody - Whitney Houston 112

I Wanna Learn a Love Song - Harry Chapin 47

I Want It That Way - Backstreet Boys 9

I Want To Break Free - Queen 80

I Want To Hold Your Hand - The Beatles 97

I Want To Know What Love Is - Foreigner 41

I Want You Back - The Jackson 5 100

I Was Here - Beyoncé 12

I Was Made For Lovin' You - KISS 59

I Will Always Love You - Whitney Houston 112

I Will Follow You Into The Dark - Death Cab For Cutie 28

I Will Survive - Gloria Gaynor 44

I Will Wait - Mumford & Sons 68

I Won't Last A Day Without You - Carpenters 22

I Write Sins Not Tragedies - Panic! at the Disco 76

I'll Be There - The Jackson 5 100

I'll Have To Say I Love You In A Song - Jim Croce 52

I'll Never Love Again - Lady Gaga 60

I'm A Believer - The Monkees 103

I'm Gonna Be (500 Miles) - The Proclaimers 103

I'm in Love with a Monster - Fifth Harmony 40

I'm Not the Only One - Sam Smith 84

I'm Too Sexy - Right Said Fred 82

I'm With You - Avirl Lavigne 8

Ice Ice Baby - Vanilla Ice 111

IDGAF - Dua Lipa 32

idontwanttobeyouanymore - Billie Eilish 14

If I Ain't Got You - Alicia Keys 6

If I Can Dream - Elvis Presley 37

If I Fell - The Beatles 97

If I Had A Million Dollars - Barenaked Ladies 11

If I Let You Go - Westlife 111

If I Were A Boy - Beyoncé 13

Illenium - Chainsmokers ft. Lennon Stella 23

Imagine - John Lennon 54

In Bloom - Nirvana 71

In My Life - Beatles 11

In My Life - The Beatles 97

Incomplete - Sisqo 90

Industry Baby - Lil Nas X ft Jack Harlow 62

Infinity - One Direction 75

Interstate Love Song - Stone Temple Pilots 92

Into the Unknown - Frozen 2 43

Iris - Goo Goo Dolls 44

Ironic - Alanis Morisette 5

Irreplaceable - Beyoncé 13

It's a Man's Man's Man's World - James Brown 51

It's All Been Done - Barenaked Ladies 11

It's All Coming Back To Me Now - Celine Dion 23

It's Gonna Be Me - *NSYNC 1

It's My Life - Bon Jovi 18

It's Now Or Never - Elvis Presley 37

It's Now Or Never - Elvis Presley 38

It's Your Love - Tim McGraw, Faith Hill 107

Jaded - Aerosmith 4

Jailhouse Rock - Elvis Presley 37

Jambalaya - Creedence Clearwater Revival 28
Jar Of Hearts - Christina Perri 25
Jealous Guy - John Lennon 54
jealousy, jealousy - Olivia Rodrigo 73
Jenny Was a Friend of Mine - The Killers 101
Jessie's Girl - Rick Springfield 82
Johnny B. Goode - Chuck Berry 25
Jolene - Dolly Parton 31
Juice - Lizzo 63
Jump Around - House Of Pain 49
Just Around The River Bend - Pocahontas 78
Just The Way You Are - Billy Joel 14
Just The Way You Are - Bruno Mars 20
Keep Your Head Up - Ben Howard 12
Kickapoo - Tenacious D 94
Kill Em With Kindness - Selena Gomez 86
Kings & Queens - Ava Max 8
Kiss - Prince 79
Kiss From a Rose - Seal 85
Kiss Me - Sixpence None The Richer 90
Kiss Me More - Doja Cat ft. SZA 31
Kiss The Girl - The Little Mermaid 102
Kiss You - One Direction 74
Kiwi - Harry Stylez 48
Knockin' On Heaven's Door - Bob Dylan 17
Kokomo - The Beach Boys 95
Kryptonite - 3 Doors Down 1
Kung Fu Fighting - Carl Douglas 22
La La Land - Demi Lovato 29
Lady In Red - Chris DeBurgh 24
Lana Del Rey - Summertime Sadness 60
Landslide - Fleetwood Mac 40
Last Christmas - Wham! 112
Last Dance - Donna Summer 32
Last Friday Night (T.G.I.F.) - Katy Perry 57
Lately - Stevie Wonder 91
Lay Me Down - Sam Smith 84
Leader of the Pack - The Shangri-Las 104
Leave The Door Open - Bruno Mars 20
Leaving On a Jet Plane - John Denver 53
Lebanese Blonde - Thievery Corporation 107
Let Go - Frou Frou 42
Let It Be - The Beatles 97
Let It Go - Frozen 42
Let's Twist Again - Chubby Checker 25
Levitating - Dua Lipa 32
Life Goes On - BTS 21
Light My Fire - The Doors 99
Light Switch - Charlie Puth 24
Lights - Ellie Goulding 35
Like A Prayer - Madonna 64
Like a Rock - Bob Seger 17
Like a Rolling Stone - Bob Dylan 16
Like a Stone - Audioslave 8
Like I Can - Sam Smith 84
Like I'm Gonnea Lose You - Meghan Trainor ft. John Legend 67
Lips Are Movin' - Meghan Trainor 66

Listen - Beyoncé 13
Listen to Your Heart - Roxette 83
Little Do You Know - Alex & Sierra 5
Little Lion Man - Mumford & Sons 68
Little Talks - Of Monsters And Men 72
Little Things - One Direction 74
Livin' On A Prayer - Bon Jovi 17
Livin' On A Prayer - Bon Jovi 18
Livin' Thing - Electric Light Orchestra 34
Locked Out Of Heaven - Bruno Mars 20
Lonely Day - System of a Down 93
Look What You Made Me Do - Taylor Swift 94
Lookin' Out My Back Door - Creedence Clearwater Revival 27
Lose You To Love Me - Selena Gomez 86
Lose Yourself - Eminem 38
Losing My Religion - R.E.M. 80
Lost Boy - Ruth B 83
Love Again - Dua Lipa 33
Love is a Battlefield - Pat Benatar 77
Love Is An Open Door - Frozen 43
Love Me Like You Do - Ellie Goulding 35
Love Of My Life - Queen 80
Love On The Brain - Rihanna 82
Love On Top - Beyoncé 13
Love Shack - B-52's 9
Love Song - Sara Bareilles 84
Love Story - Taylor Swift 94
Love The Way You Lie - Eminem & Rihanna 38
Love You Goodbye - One Direction 75
Love You Like A Love Song - Selena Gomez 86
Love Yourself - Justin Bieber 55
Lovebug - The Jonas Brothers 101
Lovefool - The Cardigans 98
lovely - Billie Eilish 14
lovely (with Khalid) - Billie Eilish 14
Lover - Taylor Swift 94
Low - Flo Rida, T-Pain 41
Lucid Dreams - Juice WRLD 55
Lucky - Britney Spears 19
Lucky - Jason Mraz, Colbie Caillat 51
Mad World - Gary Jules 43
Made You Look - Meghan Trainor 66
Make You Feel My Love - Adele 2
Mama Mia - ABBA 2
Mambo No. 5 - Lou Bega 63
Man in the Mirror - Michael Jackson 67
Man on the Moon - R.E.M. 80
Man! I Feel Like A Woman - Shania Twain 87
Maneater - Hall & Oates 46
Marry You - Bruno Mars 20
Masterpiece - Jessie J 52
Material Girl - Madonna 64
Matilda - Harry Stylez 48
Me Too - Meghan Trainor 66
Mercy - Shawn Mendes 87
Migraine - twenty one pilots 110
Million Reasons - Lady Gaga 60

Mirrors - Justin Timberlake 56
Miss Movin' On - Fifth Harmony 40
MMMBop - Hanson 47
Mockingbird - Eminem 38
Money - Pink Floyd 78
Montero (Call Me By Your Name) - Lil Nas X 62
Moon River - Audrey Hepburn 8
More Than a Feeling - Boston 18
More Than This - One Direction 74
Moscow Mule - Bad Bunny 10
Mr. Blue Sky - Electric Light Orchestra 34
Mr. Bojangles - Nitty Gritty Dirt Band 72
Mr. Brightside - The Killers 101
Mr. Jones - Counting Crows 26
Mrs. Robinson - Simon & Garfunkel 89
My Boo - Usher, Alicia Keys 110
My Boyfriend's Back - The Angels 95
My Cheri Amour - Stevie Wonder 91
My Happy Ending - Avirl Lavigne 9
My Heart Will Go On - Celine Dion 22
My House - Flo Rida 40
My Sacrifice - Creed 26
My Way - Frank Sinatra 41
Mykonos - Fleet Foxes 40
Neon Lights - Demi Lovato 30
New Rules - Dua Lipa 33
New Slang - The Shins 104
New York, New York - Frank Sinatra 41
Night Changes - One Direction 74
Night Moves - Bob Seger 17
Nine in the Afternoon - Panic! at the Disco 76
No - Meghan Trainor 66
No Judgement - Niall Horan 70
No One - Alicia Keys 6
No One's Gonna Love You - Band of Horses 10
No Sleep Till Brooklyn - Beastie Boys 11
Nothing Compares 2 U - Sinead O'Connor 90
Nothing Else Matters - Metallica 67
Nothing's Gonna Stop Us Now - Starship 90
November Rain - Guns N' Roses 46
O-o-h Child - The Five Stairsteps 99
Ob-La-Di, Ob-La-Da - The Beatles 97
Oh, Pretty Woman - Roy Orbison 83
Old TIme Rock & Roll - Bob Seger 17
Old Town Road - Lil Nas X 62
On My Mind - Ellie Goulding 35
One Call Away - Charlie Puth 24
One Last Breath - Creed 27
One Last Cry - Brian McKnight 18
One Last Time - Ariana Grande 7
One of These Things First - Nick Drake 70
One Way Or Another - Blondie 15
One Week - Barenaked Ladies 11
Only Happy When It Rains - Garbage 43
Only Human - Jonas Brothers 55
Only The Lonely - Roy Orbison 83
Only You (And You Alone) - The Platters 103

Oops!... I Did it Again - Britney Spears 19
Otherside - Red Hot Chili Peppers 81
Our Lips Are Sealed - The Go-Go's 100
Over The Rainbow / What a Wonderful World - Israel Kamakawiwo'ole 50
Paint It Black - Rolling Stones 83
Panini - Lil Nas X 62
Papa's Got A Brand New Bag - James Brown 50
Paparazzi - Lady Gaga 60
Paris - Chainsmokers 23
Part of Your World - The Little Mermaid 102
Party In The USA - Miley Cyrus 68
Patience - Guns N' Roses 45
Perfect - Ed Sheeran 33
Permission to Dance - BTS 21
Personal Jesus - Depeche Mode 30
Photograph - Ed Sheeran 34
Photograph - Nickelback 71
Piano Man - Billy Joel 15
Piece By Piece - Kelly Clarkson 59
Pinball Wizard - The Who 106
Please Forgive Me - Bryan Adams 21
Plush - Stone Temple Pilots 92
Pokemon - Theme Song 107
Praying - Ke$ha 58
Praying - Sam Smith 84
Pretty Hurts - Beyoncé 12
Price Tag - Jessie J ft. B.o.B 52
Prince Ali - Aladdin 4
Proud Mary - Creedence Clearwater Revival 27
Purple Haze - Jimi Hendrix 53
Purple Rain - Prince 79
Put Your Head On My Shoulder - Paul Anka 77
Quit Playing Games With My Heart - Backstreet Boys 10
Radioactive - Imagine Dragons 50
Raindrops Keep Falling on My Head - B.J. Thomas 9
Raise Your Glass - P!nk 75
Red Red Wine - UB40 110
Reflection - Mulan 68
Rehab - Amy Winehouse 6
Rhythm of the Rain - The Cascades 98
Ride - twenty one pilots 109
Riders on the Storm - The Doors 99
Right Round - Flo Rida, Ke$ha 41
Ring of Fire - Johnny Cash 54
Riptide - Vance Joy 111
Roar - Katy Perry 57
Rock and Roll All Nite - KISS 59
Rocket Man - Elton John 37
Rockstar - Nickelback 71
Rolling in the Deep - Adele 3
Roses - Chainsmokers ft. Rozes 23
Roxanne - The Police 103
Rude - Magic! 65
Rumor Has It - Adele 3
Runaway - Del Shannon 29
Running Up That Hill - Kate Bush 56
Same Love - Macklemore & Ryan Lewis 64

Same Old Love - Selena Gomez 86
Sanctuary - Joji 55
Satisfaction - Rolling Stones 82
Save A Horse Ride A Cowboy - Big & Rich 14
Saving All My Love For You - Whitney Houston 112
Say it Ain't So - Weezer 111
Say My Name - Destiny's Child 30
Say So - Doja Cat 31
Scar Tissue - Red Hot Chili Peppers 81
Season of the Witch - Donovan 32
Seasons of Love - Rent 82
See You Again - Wiz Khalifa ft. Charlie Puth 112
Semi-Charmed Life - Third Eye Blind 107
Senorita - Shawn Mendes, Camila Cabello 88
September - Earth, Wind and Fire 33
Set Fire To The Rain - Adele 3
Seven Nation Army - The White Stripes 106
Sexual Healing - Marvin Gaye 66
Shake It Off - Taylor Swift 94
Shake Your Groove Thing - Peaches & Herb 77
Shallow - Lady Gaga, Bradley Cooper 60
Shape of My Heart - Sting 91
Shape Of My Heart - Backstreet Boys 10
Shape of You - Ed Sheeran 34
Sharks - Imagine Dragons 50
She Has No Time - Keane 58
She Used to Be Mine - Sara Bareilles 85
She Will Be Loved - Maroon 5 66
Sherry - Frankie Valli and the Four Seasons 42
Shine On You Crazy Diamond - Pink Floyd 78
Should I Stay Or Should I Go - The Clash 98
Show Me The Meaning Of Being Lonely - Backstreet Boys 9
Sign Of The Times - Harry Styles 48
Signed, Sealed, Delivered I'm Yours - Stevie Wonder 91
Simple Man - Lynyrd Skynyrd 64
Since U Been Gone - Kelly Clarkson 59
Single Ladies - Beyoncé 12
Single Ladies - Beyoncé 13
Sister Golden Hair - America 6
Sk8er Boi - Avirl Lavigne 9
Skinny Love - Birdy 14
Skyscraper - Demi Lovato 29
Slow Down - Selena Gomez 86
Slow Hands - Niall Horan 70
Smells Like Teen Spirit - Nirvana 71
Smile Like You Mean It - The Killers 101
Smooth Criminal - Michael Jackson 67
Snowman - Sia 88
So Am I - Ava Max 8
So Good - Halsey 47
So What - P!nk 75
Sober - P!nk 76
Some Nights - Fun 43
Somebody That I Used To Know - Elliot Smith 35
Somebody That I Used To Know - Gotye and Kimbra 44
Somebody To Love - Queen 80
Somebody Told Me - The Killers 101

Someone Like You - Adele 3
Someone You Loved - Lewis Capaldi 61
Something To Believe In - Poison 79
Sometimes - Britney Spears 19
Somewhere Only We Know - Keane 58
Somewhere Over the Rainbow - Judy Garland 55
Somthing Just Like This - Chainsmokers ft. Coldplay 23
Son of Sam - Elliot Smith 36
Sorry - Justin Bieber 55
SOS - The Jonas Brothers 100
Sour Girl - Stone Temple Pilots 92
Speechless - Naomi Scott 69
Spirit in the Sky - Norman Greenbaum 72
Stairway To Heaven - Led Zeppelin 61
Stan - Eminem ft Dido 39
Stand By Me - Ben E. King 12
Starlight - Muse 69
Starships - Nick Minaj 71
Stay - Rihanna, Mikky Ekko 82
Stay With Me - Sam Smith 84
Stayin' Alive - Bee Gees 12
Steal My Girl - One Direction 74
Still Falling For You - Ellie Goulding 35
Stitches - Shawn Mendes 88
Stone Cold - Demi Lovato 29
Story Of My Life - One Direction 74
Strangers In The Night - Frank Sinatra 41
Streets - Doja Cat 31
Stressed Out - twenty one pilots 109
Stronger - Britney Spears 19
Stuck On You - Lionel Richie 62
Such Great Height - The Postal Service 103
Sucker - Jonas Brothers 55
Suddenly I See - KT Tunstall 59
Sugar - Maroon 5 65
Sugar Sugar - The Archies 95
Summer Nights - Grease 45
Sun Goes Down - Lil Nas X 62
Sunday Morning - Maroon 5 65
Sunday, Bloody Sunday - U2 110
Sunflower - Post Malone, Swae Lee 79
Super Bass - Nick Minaj 70
Super Freaky Girl - Nick Minaj 71
Superstition - Stevie Wonder 91
Surfin' USA - The Beach Boys 96
Suspicious Minds - Elvis Presley 37
Sway - Dean Martin 28
Sweet Baby James - James Taylor 51
Sweet But Psycho - Ava Max 8
Sweet Caroline - Neil Diamond 69
Sweet Child of Mine - Guns N' Roses 46
Sweet Creatures - Harry Stylez 48
Sweet Dreams - Eurythmics 39
Sweet Home Alabama - Lynrd Skynrd 64
Take a Chance on Me - ABBA 2
Take It Easy - Eagles 33
Take Me Home, Country Roads - John Denver 53

Take Me Out - Franz Ferdinand 42
Take Me To Church - Hozier 49
Take On Me - a-ha 2
Tale As Old As Time - Beauty And The Beast 11
Talking To The Moon - Bruno Mars 20
Tattooed Heart - Ariana Grande 7
Taxi - Harry Chapin 48
Tear in My Heart - twenty one pilots 110
Tearin' Up My Heart - *NSYNC 1
Tears in Heaven - Eric Clapton 39
Teenager in Love - Dion & The Belmonts 31
Tennessee Whiskey - Chris Stapleton 24
Test Drive - Joji 54
Thank God I'm a Country Boy - John Denver 53
Thank You For Loving Me - Bon Jovi 18
That Funny Feeling - Bo Burnham 16
That Thing You Do - The Wonders 106
That'll Be The Day - Buddy Holly 21
That's All Right - Elvis Presley 38
That's Hilarious - Charlie Puth 24
That's The Way (I Like It) - KC And The Sunshine Band 58
That's What I Want - Lil Nas X 62
The Aadams Family - Theme Song 107
The Ballad of Mona Lisa - Panic! at the Disco 76
The Best - Tina Turner 108
The Boys are Back in Town - Thin Lizzy 107
The Cave - Mumford and Sons 69
The Climb - Miley Cyrus 68
The District Sleeps Alone Tonight - The Postal Service 103
The First Day Of My Life - Bright Eyes 19
The Fresh Prince of Bel-Air - Theme Song 107
The Funeral - Band of Horses 10
The Greatest Love Of All - Whitney Houston 112
The Hardest Button To Button - The White Stripes 106
The Joker - Steve Miller Band 91
The Lazy Song - Bruno Mars 20
The Logical Song - Supertramp 93
The Long and Winding Road - The Beatles 98
The One I Love - R.E.M. 80
The One That Got Away - Katy Perry 57
The Only Living Boy In New York - Simon & Garfunkel 89
The Party's Crashing Us - Of Montreal 72
The Real Slim Shady - Eminem 38
The Scientist - Coldplay 26
The Sound Of Silence - Simon & Garfunkel 89
The Times, They Are A-Changin' - Bob Dylan 17
The Wanderer - Dion 30
The Way I Am - Charlie Puth 24
The Way I Am - Ingrid Michaelson 50
The Way You Look Tonight - Frank Sinatra 41
The Way You Make Me Feel - Michael Jackson 67
There Are Worse Things I Could Do - Grease 45
There Is A Light That Never Goes Out - The Smiths 104
There's a Kind of Hush - Herman's Hermits 49
There's Nothing Holding Me Back - Shawn Mendes 88
These Dreams - Heart 49
Thinking Out Loud - Ed Sheeran 34

Thirteen - Big Star 14
This Charming Man - The Smiths 105
This Feeling - Chainsmoker ft. Kelsea Ballerini 23
This I Promise You - *NSYNC 1
This Is The Last Time - Keane 58
This is What Falling in Love Feels Like - JVKE 56
This is What Heartbreak Feels Like - JVKE 56
This Kiss - Faith Hill 39
This Love - Maroon 5 65
This Town - Niall Horan 70
Thrift Shop - Macklemore & Ryan Lewis 64
Thriller - Michael Jackson 68
Thunder - Imagine Dragons 50
Ticket To Ride - The Beatles 97
TiK ToK - Ke$ha 58
Till There Was You - The Beatles 98
Timber - Pitbull and Ke$ha 78
Time In A Bottle - Jim Croce 52
Time Warp - The Rocky Horror Picture Show 104
Tiny Dancer - Elton John 36
Titanium - David Guetta ft. Sia 28
To Love Somebody - Bee Gees 12
Too Close - Alex Clare 5
Too Dumb to Die - Green Day 45
Too Good At Goodbyes - Sam Smith 84
Too Much to Ask - Niall Horan 70
Torn - Natalie Imbruglia 69
Total Eclipse Of The Heart - Bonnie Tyler 18
Touch Me - The Doors 99
Toxic - Britney Spears 19
Toxicity - System of a Down 93
traitor - Olivia Rodrigo 73
Treat You Better - Shawn Mendes 88
Tribute - Tenacious D 94
Truly Madly Deeply - Savage Garden 85
Truth Hurts - Lizzo 63
Try - P!nk 75
Try Everything - Shakira 87
Tubthumping - Chumbawamba 25
Turn The Page - Bob Seger 17
Turning Tables - Adele 3
Tutti Frutti - Little Richard 63
Twist And Shout - The Beatles 98
Two Weeks - Grizzly Bear 45
Unbreak My Heart - Toni Braxton 108
Unchained Melody - The Righteous Brothers 104
Uncover - Zara Larsson 112
Under The Bridge - Red Hot Chili Peppers 81
Under The Sea - The Little Mermaid 102
Underneath Your Clothes - Shakira 87
Undone (The Sweater Song) - Weezer 111
Uninvited - Alanis Morisette 5
Unstoppable - Sia 89
Unthinkable (I'm Ready) - Alicia Keys 6
Unwritten - Natasha Bedingfield 69
Upside Down - JVKE 56
Uptown Funk - Bruno Mars & Mark Ronson 20

Uptown Girl - Billy Joel 15
Vacation - The Go-Go's 100
Valerie - Amy Winehouse & Mark Ronson 7
Vaseline - Stone Temple Pilots 92
Vincent - Don McLean 32
Viva La Vida - Coldplay 26
Voodoo Child - Jimi Hendrix 53
Wake Me Up Before You Go Go - The Overtones 103
Walk Like a Man - Frankie Valli and the Four Seasons 42
Walk The Moon - Shania Twain 87
Walk This Way - Aerosmith 4
Walking On Sunshine - Katrina And The Waves 57
Waltz #2 - Elliot Smith 36
Wanted Dead Or Alive - Bon Jovi 18
Warrior - Demi Lovato 29
Waterfalls - TLC 108
Watermelon Sugar - Harry Stylez 48
We Are Never Ever Getting Back Together - Taylor Swift 94
We Are The Champions - Queen 80
We Belong - Pat Benatar 77
We Belong Together - Mariah Carey 65
We Can't Stop - Miley Cyrus 68
We Don't Talk About Bruno - Encanto 39
We Don't Talk Anymore - Selena Gomez, Charlie Puth 86
We Got the Beat - The Go-Go's 100
We Gotta Get Out of This Place - The Angels 95
We Might As Well Be Strangers - Keane 59
We Own the Night - The Wanted 105
We've Only Just Begun - Carpenters 22
Welcome to the Black Parade - My Chemical Romance 69
Welcome To The Internet - Bo Burnham 16
Welcome to the Jungle - Guns N' Roses 46
What a Day for a Daydream - Lovin' Spoonful 63
What a Wonderful World - Louis Armstrong 63
What About Us - P!nk 76
What Makes You Beautiful - One Direction 74
What's Love Got To Do With It - Tina Turner 108
What's Up - 4 Non Blondes 2
When I Look At You - Miley Cyrus 68
When I Was Your Man - Bruno Mars 20
When I'm Gone - 3 Doors Down 1
When I'm Sixty-Four - The Beatles 96
When We Were Young - Adele 3
When You're Gone - Avirl Lavigne 9
Whenever, Wherever - Shakira 87
Whistle - Flo Rida 40
White Woman's Instagram - Bo Burnham 16
Who Knew - P!nk 76
Who You Are - Jessie J 51
Wide Open Spaces - Dixie Chicks 31
Wihtout the Love - Demi Lovato 30
Wish You Were Here - Pink Floyd 78
With A Little Help From My Friends - Joe Cocker 53
With A Little Help From My Friends - The Beatles 98
With Arms Wide Open - Creed 27
With Or Without You - U2 110
Without Me - Eminem 38

Without Me - Halsey 46
Without You - Mariah Carey 65
Wolves - Selena Gomez, Marshmello 86
Woman - Doja Cat 31
Womanizer - Britney Spears 19
Wonderful Tonight - Eric Clapton 39
Wonderwall - Oasis 72
Work From Home - Fifth Harmony ft. Ty Dolla Sign 40
Worth It - Fifth Harmony 39
Wouldn't It Be Nice - The Beach Boys 95
Wreck of the Edmund Fitzgerald - Gordon Lightfoot 44
Wrecking Ball - Miley Cyrus 68
Writing's On The Wall - Sam Smith 84
Year 3000 - The Jonas Brothers 101
Yellow - Coldplay 26
Yesterday - The Beatles 97
YMCA - Village People 111
Yonaguni - Bad Bunny 10
You And I - Ingrid Michaelson 50
You Are My Destiny - Paul Anka 77
You Are The Reason - Calum Scott 21
You Belong With Me - Taylor Swift 94
You Can Call Me Al - Simon & Garfunkel 89
You Can't Always Get What You Want - Rolling Stones 82
You Don't Have To Say You Love Me - Dusty Springfield 33
You Give Love a Bad Name - Bon Jovi 18
You Got It - Roy Orbison 83
You Haven't Seen The Last Of Me - Cher 24
You Know I'm No Good - Amy Winehouse 6
You Make My Dreams Come True - Hall/Oates 46
You Never Can Tell - Chuck Berry 25
You Oughta Know - Alanis Morisette 5
You Really Got Me - The Kinks 101
You Right - Doja Cat, The Weeknd 31
You Should Be Sad - Halsey 46
You'll Be in My Heart - Tarzan 93
You're Beautiful - James Blunt 50
You're My World - Tom Jones 108
You're So Vain - Carly Simon 22
You're Still The One I Want - Shania Twain 87
You're The One That I Want - Grease 45
Your Cheatin' Heart - Hank Williams, Jr. 47
Your Song - Elton John 36
Ziggy Stardust - David Bowie 28
Zombie - The Cranberries 99

*NSYNC	*NSYNC	*NSYNC
Tearin' Up My Heart	This I Promise You	It's Gonna Be Me

*NSYNC	*NSYNC	21 Savage
Bye Bye Bye	God Must Have Spent A Little More Time On You	Bank Account

3 Doors Down	3 Doors Down	3 Doors Down
Here Without You	Kryptonite	When I'm Gone

1

4 Non Blondes	a-ha	ABBA
What's Up	Take On Me	Dancing Queen

ABBA	ABBA	ABBA
Mama Mia	Chiquitita	Fernando

ABBA	AC/DC	Adele
Take a Chance on Me	Dirty Deeds Done Dirt Cheap	Make You Feel My Love

2

Adele	Adele	Adele
Someone Like You	Set Fire To The Rain	When We Were Young

Adele	Adele	Adele
Turning Tables	Hello	Easy On Me

Adele	Adele	Aerosmith
Rolling in the Deep	Rumor Has It	I Don't Wanna Miss A Thing

Aerosmith	Aerosmith	Aerosmith
Jaded	Walk This Way	Cryin'

Aerosmith	Air Supply	Air Supply
Dream On	All Out of Love	Chances

Aladdin	Aladdin	Alan Walker
Prince Ali	A Whole New World	Faded

4

Alanis Morisette	Alanis Morisette	Alanis Morisette
Ironic	You Oughta Know	Hand In My Pocket

Alanis Morisette	Alanis Morisette	Alessia Cara
Head Over Feet	Uninvited	How Far I'll Go

Alex & Sierra	Alex Clare	Alicia Keys
Little Do You Know	Too Close	Girl On Fire

Alicia Keys	Alicia Keys	Alicia Keys
If I Ain't Got You	No One	Fallin'

Alicia Keys	America	America
Unthinkable (I'm Ready)	A Horse With No Name	Sister Golden Hair

Amy Winehouse	Amy Winehouse	Amy Winehouse
Rehab	Back to Black	You Know I'm No Good

Amy Winehouse & Mark Ronson	Anne Murray	Aqua
Valerie	I Just Fall In Love Again	Barbie Girl

Aretha Franklin	Ariana Grande	Ariana Grande
I Say a Little Prayer	Dangerous Woman	7 Rings

Ariana Grande	Ariana Grande	Ariana Grande
One Last Time	Breathin'	Tattooed Heart

Ariana Grande, John Legend	Audioslave	Audrey Hepburn
Beauty & The Beast	**Like a Stone**	**Moon River**

Auli'i Cravalho	Ava Max	Ava Max
How Far I'll Go	**Kings & Queens**	**Sweet But Psycho**

Ava Max	Avirl Lavigne	Avirl Lavigne
So Am I	**Complicated**	**I'm With You**

Avirl Lavigne	Avirl Lavigne	Avirl Lavigne
Sk8er Boi	**My Happy Ending**	**Girlfriend**

Avirl Lavigne	B-52's	B.J. Thomas
When You're Gone	**Love Shack**	**Raindrops Keep Falling on My Head**

Backstreet Boys	Backstreet Boys	Backstreet Boys
I Want It That Way	**As Long As You Love Me**	**Show Me The Meaning Of Being Lonely**

Backstreet Boys

Everybody (Backstreet's Back)

Backstreet Boys

Shape Of My Heart

Backstreet Boys

All I Have To Give

Backstreet Boys

Quit Playing Games With My Heart

Bad Bunny

Yonaguni

Bad Bunny

Moscow Mule

Bad Bunny

Callaíta

Band of Horses

The Funeral

Band of Horses

No One's Gonna Love You

Barenaked Ladies	Barenaked Ladies	Barenaked Ladies
It's All Been Done	One Week	If I Had A Million Dollars

Barenaked Ladies	Beastie Boys	Beastie Boys
Alcohol	Fight For Your Right	No Sleep Till Brooklyn

Beatles	Beauty And The Beast	Beauty And The Beast
In My Life	Tale As Old As Time	Belle

Beauty And The Beast

Be Our Guest

Bee Gees

Stayin' Alive

Bee Gees

To Love Somebody

Ben E. King

Stand By Me

Ben Howard

Keep Your Head Up

Beyoncé

Single Ladies

Beyoncé

Pretty Hurts

Beyoncé

Cuff It

Beyoncé

I Was Here

Beyoncé	Beyoncé	Beyoncé
Break My Soul	Halo	Listen

Beyoncé	Beyoncé	Beyoncé
Single Ladies	Love On Top	If I Were A Boy

Beyoncé	Beyoncé ft Jay-Z	Beyoncé ft Jay-Z
Irreplaceable	Drunk In Love	Hey

Big & Rich	Big Star	Bill Medley, Jennifer Warnes
Save A Horse Ride A Cowboy	**Thirteen**	**(I've Had) The Time Of My Life**

Billie Eilish	Billie Eilish	Billie Eilish
idontwanttobeyouanymore	**lovely**	**lovely (with Khalid)**

Billie Eilish	Birdy	Billy Joel
i love you	**Skinny Love**	**Just The Way You Are**

14

Billy Joel	Billy Joel	Blondie
Piano Man	Uptown Girl	Heart of Glass

Blondie	Blue Öyster Cult	Blue Swede, Bjorn Skifs
One Way Or Another	Don't Fear the Reaper	Hooked on a Feeling

Bo Burnham	Bo Burnham	Bo Burnham
All Eyes On Me	Comedy	Goodbye (Possible Ending Song)

Bo Burnham	Bo Burnham	Bo Burnham
That Funny Feeling	Welcome To The Internet	Bezos 1

Bo Burnham	Bo Burnham	Bo Burnham
Bezos 2	Content	White Woman's Instagram

Bo Burnham	Bob Dylan	Bob Dylan
"1985"	Like a Rolling Stone	Hey, Mr. Tambourine Man

Bob Dylan

The Times, They Are A-Changin'

Bob Dylan

Knockin' On Heaven's Door

Bob Seger

Turn The Page

Bob Seger

Against The Wind

Bob Seger

Night Moves

Bob Seger

Old TIme Rock & Roll

Bob Seger

Like a Rock

Bon Jovi

Livin' On A Prayer

Bon Jovi

Always

Bon Jovi	Bon Jovi	Bon Jovi
Thank You For Loving Me	**It's My Life**	**Wanted Dead Or Alive**

Bon Jovi	Bon Jovi	Bonnie Tyler
You Give Love a Bad Name	**Livin' On A Prayer**	**Total Eclipse Of The Heart**

Boston	Brian McKnight	Brian McKnight
More Than a Feeling	**One Last Cry**	**Back At One**

Bright Eyes The First Day Of My Life 	Britney Spears Oops!... I Did it Again 	Britney Spears ...Baby One More Time 
Britney Spears Toxic 	Britney Spears Sometimes 	Britney Spears Everytime 
Britney Spears Lucky 	Britney Spears Womanizer 	Britney Spears Stronger 

Bruno Mars When I Was Your Man 	Bruno Mars Leave The Door Open 	Bruno Mars Locked Out Of Heaven 
Bruno Mars Grenade 	Bruno Mars The Lazy Song 	Bruno Mars Just The Way You Are 
Bruno Mars Marry You 	Bruno Mars Talking To The Moon 	Bruno Mars & Mark Ronson Uptown Funk 

Bryan Adams	Bryan Adams	BTS
Everything I Do (I Do It For You)	Please Forgive Me	Dynamite

BTS	BTS	BTS
Permission to Dance	Butter	Life Goes On

Buddy Holly	Bush	Calum Scott
That'll Be The Day	Glycerine	You Are The Reason

21

Camila Cabello ft. Young Thug

Havana

Carl Douglas

Kung Fu Fighting

Carly Rae Jepsen

Call Me Maybe

Carly Simon

You're So Vain

Carpenters

We've Only Just Begun

Carpenters

I Won't Last A Day
Without You

Carrie Underwood

Before He Cheats

Cascada

Every Time We Touch

Celine Dion

My Heart Will Go On

Celine Dion

It's All Coming Back To Me Now

Chainsmoker ft. Kelsea Ballerini

This Feeling

Chainsmokers

Paris

Chainsmokers ft. Coldplay

Somthing Just Like This

Chainsmokers ft. Daya

Don't Let Me Down

Chainsmokers ft. Halsey

Closer

Chainsmokers ft. Lennon Stella

Illenium

Chainsmokers ft. Phoebe Ryan

All We Know

Chainsmokers ft. Rozes

Roses

Charlie Puth	Charlie Puth	Charlie Puth
One Call Away	**Attention**	**How Long**

Charlie Puth	Charlie Puth	Charlie Puth
That's Hilarious	**Light Switch**	**The Way I Am**

Cher	Chris DeBurgh	Chris Stapleton
You Haven't Seen The Last Of Me	**Lady In Red**	**Tennessee Whiskey**

Christina Aguilera	Christina Aguilera	Christina Aguilera
Hurt	Genie In A Bottle	Beautiful

Christina Perri	Christina Perri	Chubby Checker
A Thousand Years	Jar Of Hearts	Let's Twist Again

Chuck Berry	Chuck Berry	Chumbawamba
Johnny B. Goode	You Never Can Tell	Tubthumping

Colbie Caillat	Coldplay	Coldplay
Bubbly	Fix You	The Scientist

Coldplay	Coldplay	Coldplay
Yellow	Viva La Vida	Don't Panic

Commodores	Counting Crows	Creed
Easy	Mr. Jones	My Sacrifice

26

Creed	Creed	Creed
Higher	One Last Breath	With Arms Wide Open

Creedence Clearwater Revival	Creedence Clearwater Revival	Creedence Clearwater Revival
Lookin' Out My Back Door	Have You Ever Seen the Rain	Proud Mary

Creedence Clearwater Revival	Creedence Clearwater Revival	Creedence Clearwater Revival
Bad Moon Rising	I Heard It Through The Grapevine	Fortunate Son

Creedence Clearwater Revival

Jambalaya

Crowded House

Don't Dream It's Over

Cults

Always Forever

Cyndi Lauper

Girls Just Want To Have Fun

Daniel Powter

Bad Day

David Bowie

Ziggy Stardust

David Guetta ft. Sia

Titanium

Dean Martin

Sway

Death Cab For Cutie

I Will Follow You Into The Dark

Del Shannon	Demi Lovato	Demi Lovato
Runaway	Heart Attack	Stone Cold

Demi Lovato	Demi Lovato	Demi Lovato
La La Land	Skyscraper	Don't Forget

Demi Lovato	Demi Lovato	Demi Lovato
Warrior	Give Your Heart a Break	Anyone

Demi Lovato
Wihtout the Love

Demi Lovato
Neon Lights

Depeche Mode
Personal Jesus

Depeche Mode
Enjoy the Silence

Destiny's Child
Bootylicious

Destiny's Child
Say My Name

Destiny's Child
Emotion

Dexy's Midnight Runners
Come on Eileen

Dion
The Wanderer

Dion & The Belmonts	Dixie Chicks	DNCE
Teenager in Love	Wide Open Spaces	Cake by the Ocean

Doja Cat	Doja Cat	Doja Cat
Streets	Say So	Woman

Doja Cat ft. SZA	Doja Cat, The Weeknd	Dolly Parton
Kiss Me More	You Right	Jolene

Dolly Parton	Don McLean	Don McLean
9 To 5	Vincent	American Pie

Donna Lewis	Donna Summer	Donna Summer
I Love You Always Forever	Last Dance	Hot Stuff

Donovan	Dua Lipa	Dua Lipa
Season of the Witch	Levitating	IDGAF

Dua Lipa	Dua Lipa	Dua Lipa
New Rules	Don't Start Now	Love Again

Dua Lipa	Dusty Springfield	Eagles
Break My Heart	You Don't Have To Say You Love Me	Take It Easy

Eagles	Earth, Wind and Fire	Ed Sheeran
Hotel California	September	Perfect

Ed Sheeran

Shape of You

Ed Sheeran

Thinking Out Loud

Ed Sheeran

Photograph

Ed Sheeran

Bad Habits

Edward Sharpe & The Magnetic Zeros

Home

Eiffel 65

Blue

Electric Light Orchestra

Mr. Blue Sky

Electric Light Orchestra

Don't Bring Me Down

Electric Light Orchestra

Livin' Thing

Ellie Goulding	Ellie Goulding	Ellie Goulding
Love Me Like You Do	Burn	Lights

Ellie Goulding	Ellie Goulding	Ellie Goulding
Still Falling For You	On My Mind	Army

Elliot Smith	Elliot Smith	Elliot Smith
Between the Bars	Angeles	Somebody That I Used To Know

Elliot Smith

A Fond Farewell

Elliot Smith

Waltz #2

Elliot Smith

Son of Sam

Elliot Smith

Everything Reminds Me
of Her

Elton John

Your Song

Elton John

Tiny Dancer

Elton John

Don't Let The Sun Go
Down On Me

Elton John

I Guess That's Why They
Call It The Blues

Elton John

Bennie And The Jets

Elton John

Don't Go Breaking My Heart

Elton John

Rocket Man

Elton John

Crocodile Rock

Elvis Presley

It's Now Or Never

Elvis Presley

Can't Help Falling In Love

Elvis Presley

If I Can Dream

Elvis Presley

Jailhouse Rock

Elvis Presley

Hound Dog

Elvis Presley

Suspicious Minds

Elvis Presley

Don't Be Cruel

Elvis Presley

That's All Right

Elvis Presley

It's Now Or Never

Elvis Presley

Always On My Mind

Eminem

Lose Yourself

Eminem

Without Me

Eminem

The Real Slim Shady

Eminem

Mockingbird

Eminem & Rihanna

Love The Way You Lie

Eminem ft Dido Stan 	Encanto We Don't Talk About Bruno 	Enrique Iglesias Hero 
Eric Clapton Tears in Heaven 	Eric Clapton Wonderful Tonight 	Eurythmics Sweet Dreams 
Everly Brothers Crying In The Rain 	Faith Hill This Kiss 	Fifth Harmony Worth It 

Fifth Harmony

I'm in Love with a Monster

Fifth Harmony

Miss Movin' On

Fifth Harmony

Bo$$

Fifth Harmony ft. Ty Dolla Sign

Work From Home

Fleet Foxes

Mykonos

Fleetwood Mac

Landslide

Flo Rida

Whistle

Flo Rida

My House

Flo Rida

Good Feeling

Flo Rida, David Guetta	Flo Rida, Ke$ha	Flo Rida, T-Pain
Club Can't Handle Me	**Right Round**	**Low**

Foreigner	Frank Sinatra	Frank Sinatra
I Want To Know What Love Is	**Strangers In The Night**	**New York, New York**

Frank Sinatra	Frank Sinatra	Frank Sinatra
The Way You Look Tonight	**Fly Me To The Moon**	**My Way**

Frank Sinatra

Come Fly With Me

Frankie Valli and the Four Seasons

I Can't Take My Eyes Off You

Frankie Valli and the Four Seasons

Sherry

Frankie Valli and the Four Seasons

Bye Bye Baby (Baby Goodbye)

Frankie Valli and the Four Seasons

Walk Like a Man

Franz Ferdinand

Take Me Out

Frou Frou

Let Go

Frozen

Let It Go

Frozen

For The First Time In Forever

42

Frozen Love Is An Open Door 	Frozen 2 Into the Unknown 	Frozen 2 All is Found 
Fun Some Nights 	Garbage Only Happy When It Rains 	Gary Jules Mad World 
GAYLE abcdefu 	Gazebo I Like Chopin 	George Ezra Budapest 

George Michael

Faith

Gloria Gaynor

I Will Survive

Gnarls Barkely

Crazy

Goo Goo Dolls

Iris

Gordon Lightfoot

Wreck of the Edmund Fitzgerald

Gorillaz

Feel Good, Inc

Gorillaz

Clint Eastwood

Gotye and Kimbra

Somebody That I Used To Know

Grace VanderWaal

I Don't Know My Name

Grease	Grease	Grease
There Are Worse Things I Could Do	You're The One That I Want	Hopelessly Devoted To You

Grease	Green Day	Green Day
Summer Nights	Good Riddance (Time of Your Life)	Too Dumb to Die

Grizzly Bear	Guns N' Roses	Guns N' Roses
Two Weeks	Patience	Don't Cry

Guns N' Roses
November Rain

Guns N' Roses
Welcome to the Jungle

Guns N' Roses
Sweet Child of Mine

Hall & Oates
Maneater

Hall/Oates
You Make My Dreams Come True

Halsey
Without Me

Halsey
Bad at Love

Halsey
You Should Be Sad

Halsey
Colors

Halsey	Halsey	Halsey
Gasoline	So Good	Castle

Halsey	Hank Williams, Jr.	Hanson
Eyes Closed	Your Cheatin' Heart	MMMBop

Harry Chapin	Harry Chapin	Harry Chapin
Cat's In The Cradle	I Wanna Learn a Love Song	Better Place To Be

Harry Chapin	Harry Styles	Harry Styles
Taxi	Sign Of The Times	Falling

Harry Styles	Harry Stylez	Harry Stylez
As It Was	Sweet Creatures	Kiwi

Harry Stylez	Harry Stylez	Harry Stylez
Watermelon Sugar	Adore You	Matilda

Harry Stylez	Harvey Danger	Heart
Boyfriends	Flagpole Sitta	These Dreams

Hercules	Herman's Hermits	House Of Pain
Go the Distance	There's a Kind of Hush	Jump Around

Hozier	Imagine Dragons	Imagine Dragons
Take Me To Church	Demons	Believer

Imagine Dragons Sharks 	Imagine Dragons Thunder 	Imagine Dragons Radioactive 
Ingrid Michaelson The Way I Am 	Ingrid Michaelson You And I 	Israel Kamakawiwo'ole Over The Rainbow / What a Wonderful World 
James Blunt You're Beautiful 	James Brown I Got You (I Feel Good) 	James Brown Papa's Got A Brand New Bag 

James Brown

It's a Man's Man's Man's World

James Brown

Get Up Offa That Thing

James Taylor

Fire and Rain

James Taylor

Sweet Baby James

Jason Mraz, Colbie Caillat

Lucky

Jax

I Know Victoria's Secret

Jeff Buckley

Hallelujah

Jessie J

Flashlight

Jessie J

Who You Are

Jessie J	Jessie J	Jessie J ft. B.o.B
Masterpiece	**Domino**	**Price Tag**

Jessie J, Ariana Grande, Nicki Minaj	Jewel	Jim Croce
Bang Bang	**Foolish Games**	**Bad Bad Leroy Brown**

Jim Croce	Jim Croce	Jim Croce
I Got a Name	**Time In A Bottle**	**I'll Have To Say I Love You In A Song**

Jimi Hendrix

All Along the Watchtower

Jimi Hendrix

Purple Haze

Jimi Hendrix

Voodoo Child

Jimmy Cliff

I Can See Clearly Now

Joan Jett

I Love Rock 'N Roll

Joe Cocker

With A Little Help From My Friends

John Denver

Take Me Home, Country Roads

John Denver

Leaving On a Jet Plane

John Denver

Thank God I'm a Country Boy

John Legend	John Lennon	John Lennon
All Of Me	Imagine	Jealous Guy

John Mellencamp	Johnny Cash	Johnny Cash
Hurts So Good	Ring of Fire	I Walk the Line

Johnny Cash	Joji	Joji
Hurt	Test Drive	Glimpse of Us

Joji	Jonas Brothers	Jonas Brothers
Sanctuary	Only Human	Sucker

Journey	Judy Garland	Juice WRLD
Don't Stop Believin'	Somewhere Over the Rainbow	Lucid Dreams

Justin Bieber	Justin Bieber	Justin Bieber
Baby	Sorry	Love Yourself

Justin Bieber	Justin Timberlake	Justin Timberlake
Boyfriend	**Can't Stop The Feeling**	**Mirrors**

JVKE	JVKE	JVKE
Upside Down	This is What Heartbreak Feels Like	Golden Hour

JVKE	Kansas	Kate Bush
This is What Falling in Love Feels Like	Dust In The Wind	Running Up That Hill

Katrina And The Waves	Katy Perry	Katy Perry
Walking On Sunshine	**Roar**	**Hot 'n' Cold**

Katy Perry	Katy Perry	Katy Perry
Firework	**Last Friday Night (T.G.I.F.)**	**E.T.**

Katy Perry	Katy Perry	Katy Perry
The One That Got Away	**I Kissed a Girl**	**Dark Horse**

KC And The Sunshine Band	Ke$ha	Ke$ha
That's The Way (I Like It)	TiK ToK	Praying

Keane	Keane	Keane
Somewhere Only We Know	This Is The Last Time	Everybody's Changing

Keane	Keane	Keane
She Has No Time	Bedshaped	Bend and Break

Keane	Kelly Clarkson	Kelly Clarkson
We Might As Well Be Strangers	**Since U Been Gone**	**Because Of You**

Kelly Clarkson	Kelly Clarkson	Kelly Clarkson
Breakaway	**A Moment Like This**	**Piece By Piece**

KISS	KISS	KT Tunstall
I Was Made For Lovin' You	**Rock and Roll All Nite**	**Suddenly I See**

KT Tunstall

Black Horse and a Cherry Tree

Lady Gaga

Bad Romance

Lady Gaga

I'll Never Love Again

Lady Gaga

Million Reasons

Lady Gaga

Paparazzi

Lady Gaga

Born This Way

Lady Gaga

Always Remember Us This Way

Lady Gaga, Bradley Cooper

Shallow

Summertime Sadness

Lana Del Rey

Lauper

Girls Just Want to Have Fun

LeAnn Rimes

How Do I Live

LeAnn Rimes

Can't Fight The Moonlight

Led Zeppelin

Stairway To Heaven

Lee Ann Womack

I Hope You Dance

Lemon Tree

Fool's Garden

Leona Lewis

Bleeding Love

Letters to Cleo

Cruel to Be Kind

Lewis Capaldi

Someone You Loved

Lil Nas X	Lil Nas X	Lil Nas X
Montero (Call Me By Your Name)	Old Town Road	That's What I Want

Lil Nas X	Lil Nas X	Lil Nas X ft Jack Harlow
Sun Goes Down	Panini	Industry Baby

Lionel Richie	Lionel Richie	Lionel Richie, Diana Ross
Hello	Stuck On You	Endless Love

Little Richard	Lizzo	Lizzo
Tutti Frutti	**Truth Hurts**	**Juice**

Lizzo ft. Ariana Grande	Lou Bega	Louis Armstrong
Good As Hell	Mambo No. 5	What a Wonderful World

Lovin' Spoonful	Lukas Graham	Luther Vandross
What a Day for a Daydream	7 Years	Dance With My Father

Lynrd Skynrd Sweet Home Alabama 	Lynrd Skynrd Free Bird 	Lynyrd Skynyrd Simple Man 
Macklemore & Ryan Lewis Downtown 	Macklemore & Ryan Lewis Can't Hold Us 	Macklemore & Ryan Lewis Thrift Shop 
Macklemore & Ryan Lewis Same Love 	Madonna Material Girl 	Madonna Like A Prayer 

Magic!	Manfred Mann	Mariah Carey
Rude	Blinded By The Light	Without You

Mariah Carey	Mariah Carey	Mariah Carey
Hero	Always Be My Baby	We Belong Together

Maroon 5	Maroon 5	Maroon 5
Sunday Morning	This Love	Sugar

Maroon 5	Maroon 5	Marvin Gaye
Beautiful Mistakes	She Will Be Loved	Sexual Healing

Marvin Gaye, Tammi Terrell	Meghan Trainor	Meghan Trainor
Ain't No Mountain High Enough	No	Me Too

Meghan Trainor	Meghan Trainor	Meghan Trainor
Lips Are Movin'	All About That Bass	Made You Look

Meghan Trainor	Meghan Trainor ft. John Legend	Metallica
Dear Future Husband	Like I'm Gonnea Lose You	Nothing Else Matters

Michael Jackson	Michael Jackson	Michael Jackson
Billie Jean	Bad	Beat It

Michael Jackson	Michael Jackson	Michael Jackson
Smooth Criminal	Man in the Mirror	The Way You Make Me Feel

Michael Jackson

Thriller

Miley Cyrus

We Can't Stop

Miley Cyrus

When I Look At You

Miley Cyrus

Wrecking Ball

Miley Cyrus

The Climb

Miley Cyrus

Party In The USA

Mulan

Reflection

Mumford & Sons

I Will Wait

Mumford & Sons

Little Lion Man

Mumford and Sons	Mumford and Sons	Muse
The Cave	Awake My Soul	Starlight

My Chemical Romance	Naomi Scott	Natalie Imbruglia
Welcome to the Black Parade	Speechless	Torn

Natasha Bedingfield	Neil Diamond	Nena
Unwritten	Sweet Caroline	99 Red Balloons

Niall Horan

Slow Hands

Niall Horan

This Town

Niall Horan

Too Much to Ask

Niall Horan

Flicker

Niall Horan

No Judgement

Nick Drake

One of These Things
First

Nick Minaj

Super Bass

Nick Minaj

Anaconda

Nick Minaj

Chun-Li

Nick Minaj	Nick Minaj	Nickelback
Starships	Super Freaky Girl	How You Remind Me

Nickelback	Nickelback	Nirvana
Rockstar	Photograph	Heart-Shaped Box

Nirvana	Nirvana	Nirvana
Smells Like Teen Spirit	In Bloom	Come As You Are

Nitty Gritty Dirt Band	No Doubt	Norman Greenbaum
Mr. Bojangles	Don't Speak	Spirit in the Sky

Oasis	Oasis	Of Monsters And Men
Champaign Supernova	Wonderwall	Little Talks

Of Montreal	OK Go	OK Go
The Party's Crashing Us	Get Over It	Here It Goes Again

Olivia Rodrigo

deja vu

Olivia Rodrigo

drivers license

Olivia Rodrigo

happier

Olivia Rodrigo

All I Want

Olivia Rodrigo

favorite crime

Olivia Rodrigo

traitor

Olivia Rodrigo

good 4 u

Olivia Rodrigo

1 step forward, 3 steps
back

Olivia Rodrigo

jealousy, jealousy

Olivia Rodrigo	One Direction	One Direction
brutal	Little Things	Story Of My Life

One Direction	One Direction	One Direction
What Makes You Beautiful	Kiss You	Night Changes

One Direction	One Direction	One Direction
Best Song Ever	More Than This	Steal My Girl

74

One Direction	One Direction	OneRepublic
Love You Goodbye	Infinity	Counting Stars

OneRepublic	Outkast	Owl City
I Ain't Worried	Hey Ya!	Fireflies

P!nk	P!nk	P!nk
Raise Your Glass	So What	Try

P!nk

Sober

P!nk

Who Knew

P!nk

What About Us

Panic! at the Disco

I Write Sins Not Tragedies

Panic! at the Disco

Death of a Bachelor

Panic! at the Disco

The Ballad of Mona Lisa

Panic! at the Disco

Nine in the Afternoon

Panic! at the Disco

Girls/Girls/Boys

Panic! at the Disco

Always

Pat Benatar	Pat Benatar	Pat Benatar
Hit Me With Your Best Shot	We Belong	Love is a Battlefield

Paul Anka	Paul Anka	Peaches & Herb
Put Your Head On My Shoulder	You Are My Destiny	Shake Your Groove Thing

Petula Clark	Pharrell Williams	Pharrell Williams
Downtown	Happy	Freedom

Pink Floyd	Pink Floyd	Pink Floyd
Wish You Were Here	**Shine On You Crazy Diamond**	**Comfortably Numb**

Pink Floyd	Pitbull and Ke$ha	Plain White T's
Money	**Timber**	**Hey There Delilah**

Pocahontas	Pocahontas	Poison
Colors Of The Wind	**Just Around The River Bend**	**Every Rose Has Its Thorn (With Lyrics)**

Poison	Portugal the Man	Post Malone
Something To Believe In	Feel it Still	Circles

Post Malone, Swae Lee	Post Malone	Prince
Sunflower	I Like You	Kiss

Prince	Queen	Queen
Purple Rain	Another One Bites the Dust	Bohemian Rhapsody

Queen	Queen	Queen
Crazy Little Thing Called Love	**Somebody To Love**	**Don't Stop Me Now**

Queen	Queen	Queen
We Are The Champions	Love Of My Life	I Want To Break Free

R.E.M.	R.E.M.	R.E.M.
Losing My Religion	Man on the Moon	The One I Love

R.E.O. Speedwagon

Can't Fight This Feeling Anymore

Rachel Platten

Fight Song

Radiohead

Fake Plastic Trees

Radiohead

Creep

Ray Charles

Hit The Road Jack

Red Hot Chili Peppers

Under The Bridge

Red Hot Chili Peppers

Otherside

Red Hot Chili Peppers

Californication

Red Hot Chili Peppers

Scar Tissue

Redbone

Come and Get Your Love

Rent

Seasons of Love

Rick Springfield

Jessie's Girl

Right Said Fred

I'm Too Sexy

Rihanna

Diamonds

Rihanna

Love On The Brain

Rihanna, Mikky Ekko

Stay

Rolling Stones

Satisfaction

Rolling Stones

You Can't Always Get What You Want

Rolling Stones	Rolling Stones	Roxette
Paint It Black	Beast of Burden	Listen to Your Heart

Roy Orbison	Roy Orbison	Roy Orbison
Oh, Pretty Woman	Crying	You Got It

Roy Orbison	Rupert Holmes	Ruth B
Only The Lonely	Escape (The Pina Colada Song)	Lost Boy

Sam Smith	Sam Smith	Sam Smith
I'm Not the Only One	**Stay With Me**	**Lay Me Down**

Sam Smith	Sam Smith	Sam Smith
Too Good At Goodbyes	**Writing's On The Wall**	**How Do You Sleep**

Sam Smith	Sam Smith	Sara Bareilles
Like I Can	**Praying**	**Love Song**

Sara Bareilles	Sara Bareilles	Sara Bareilles
Gravity	She Used to Be Mine	I Choose You

Sara Bareilles	Sara McLachlan	Savage Garden
Brave	Angel	Truly Madly Deeply

Savage Garden	Seal	Selena
I Knew I Loved You	Kiss From a Rose	Dreaming of You

Selena Gomez

Same Old Love

Selena Gomez

Lose You To Love Me

Selena Gomez

Love You Like A Love Song

Selena Gomez

Slow Down

Selena Gomez

Hands to Myself

Selena Gomez

Kill Em With Kindness

Selena Gomez, Charlie Puth

We Don't Talk Anymore

Selena Gomez, Marshmello

Wolves

Selena Gomez, Rema

Calm Down

86

Selena Gomez, The Scene	Shakira	Shakira
A Year Without Rain	Whenever, Wherever	Hips Don't Lie

Shakira	Shakira	Shania Twain
Try Everything	Underneath Your Clothes	Walk The Moon

Shania Twain	Shania Twain	Shawn Mendes
Man! I Feel Like A Woman	You're Still The One I Want	Mercy

Shawn Mendes

Treat You Better

Shawn Mendes

Stitches

Shawn Mendes

There's Nothing Holding Me Back

Shawn Mendes, Camila Cabello

Senorita

Sia

Bird Set Free

Sia

Alive

Sia

Chandelier

Sia

Cheap Thrills

Sia

Snowman

88

Sia	Sia	Sia
Unstoppable	Elastic Heart	Fire Meet Gasoline

Simon & Garfunkel	Simon & Garfunkel	Simon & Garfunkel
Cecelia	Mrs. Robinson	Bridge Over Troubled Water

Simon & Garfunkel	Simon & Garfunkel	Simon & Garfunkel
The Sound Of Silence	You Can Call Me Al	The Only Living Boy In New York

Sinead O'Connor	Sir Mix-A-Lot	Sisqo
Nothing Compares 2 U	Baby Got Back	Incomplete

Sixpence None The Richer	Smash Mouth	Soggy Bottom Boys
Kiss Me	All Star	I Am A Man of Constant Sorrow

Sonny & Cher	Starland Vocal Band	Starship
I Got You Babe	Afternoon Delight	Nothing's Gonna Stop Us Now

Steve Lacy	Steve Lacy	Steve Miller Band
Bad Habit	**Dark Red**	The Joker

Stevie Wonder	Stevie Wonder	Stevie Wonder
I Just Called To Say I Love You	Superstition	My Cheri Amour

Stevie Wonder	Stevie Wonder	Sting
Lately	Signed, Sealed, Delivered I'm Yours	Shape of My Heart

Sting	Sting	Stone Temple Pilots
Fields of Gold	**Englishman in New York**	**Plush**

Stone Temple Pilots	Stone Temple Pilots	Stone Temple Pilots
Sour Girl	**Interstate Love Song**	**Vaseline**

Sufjan Stevens	Sugar Ray	Sugar Ray
Chicago	Every Morning	Fly

Supertramp	Survivor	Sweet Dreams (are made of this)
The Logical Song	Eye Of The Tiger	Eurythmics

System of a Down	System of a Down	Tangerine Kitty
Lonely Day	Toxicity	Dumb Ways To Die

Tarzan	Taylor Swift	Taylor Swift
You'll Be in My Heart	Blank Space	"22"

Taylor Swift	Taylor Swift	Taylor Swift
Love Story	You Belong With Me	I Knew You Were Trouble

Taylor Swift	Taylor Swift	Taylor Swift
Lover	Shake It Off	Look What You Made Me Do

Taylor Swift	Tenacious D	Tenacious D
We Are Never Ever Getting Back Together	Kickapoo	Tribute

94

The Angels
We Gotta Get Out of This Place

The Angels
My Boyfriend's Back

The Animals
Don't Let Me Be Misunderstood

The Archies
Sugar Sugar

The Beach Boys
Wouldn't It Be Nice

The Beach Boys
Help Me, Rhonda

The Beach Boys
Kokomo

The Beach Boys
Fun, Fun, Fun

The Beach Boys
California Girls

The Beach Boys

Don't Worry Baby

The Beach Boys

Surfin' USA

The Beach Boys

I Get Around

The Beach Boys

God Only Knows

The Beatles

Blackbird

The Beatles

Don't Let Me Down

The Beatles

Hey Jude

The Beatles

Here Comes The Sun

The Beatles

When I'm Sixty-Four

The Beatles	The Beatles	The Beatles
In My Life	I Saw Her Standing There	Yesterday

The Beatles	The Beatles	The Beatles
If I Fell	Ticket To Ride	I Want To Hold Your Hand

The Beatles	The Beatles	The Beatles
Let It Be	Ob-La-Di, Ob-La-Da	Come Together

The Beatles

And I Love Her

The Beatles

Eleanor Rigby

The Beatles

Till There Was You

The Beatles

With A Little Help From My Friends

The Beatles

Twist And Shout

The Beatles

The Long and Winding Road

The Cardigans

Lovefool

The Cascades

Rhythm of the Rain

The Clash

Should I Stay Or Should I Go

The Clash	The Cranberries	The Cranberries
I Fought The Law	Dreams	Zombie

The Divinyls	The Doors	The Doors
I Touch Myself	Light My Fire	Touch Me

The Doors	The Doors	The Five Stairsteps
Riders on the Storm	Break on Through	O-o-h Child

The Flaming Lips	The Go-Go's	The Go-Go's
Do You Realize	Vacation	Our Lips Are Sealed

The Go-Go's	The Jackson 5	The Jackson 5
We Got the Beat	ABC	I'll Be There

The Jackson 5	The Jonas Brothers	The Jonas Brothers
I Want You Back	Burnin' Up	SOS

The Jonas Brothers	The Jonas Brothers	The Killers
Lovebug	Year 3000	Mr. Brightside

The Killers	The Killers	The Killers
All These Things That I've Done	Somebody Told Me	Smile Like You Mean It

The Killers	The Killers	The Kinks
Human	Jenny Was a Friend of Mine	You Really Got Me

The Lion King

Can You Feel The Love Tonight

The Lion King

I Just Can't Wait to Be King

The Lion King

Hakuna Matata

The Little Mermaid

Part of Your World

The Little Mermaid

Kiss The Girl

The Little Mermaid

Under The Sea

The Lovin' Spoonful

Do You Believe in Magic?

The Mamas and the Papas

Dream a Little Dream of Me

The Mommas and the Papas

California Dreamin'

The Monkees	The Monkees	The Overtones
I'm A Believer	Daydream Believer	Wake Me Up Before You Go Go

The Platters	The Police	The Postal Service
Only You (And You Alone)	Roxanne	Such Great Height

The Postal Service	The Proclaimers	The Ramones
The District Sleeps Alone Tonight	I'm Gonna Be (500 Miles)	I Wanna Be Sedated

The Ramones

Blitzkrieg Bop

The Righteous Brothers

Unchained Melody

The Rocky Horror Picture Show

Time Warp

The Rolling Stones

Gimme Shelter

The Ronettes

Be My Baby

The Shangri-Las

Leader of the Pack

The Shins

Caring is Creepy

The Shins

New Slang

The Smiths

There Is A Light That Never Goes Out

104

The Smiths

This Charming Man

The Smiths

Heaven Knows I'm Miserable Now

The Smiths

How Soon Is Now

The Verve

Bitter Sweet Symphony

The Wanted

Glad You Came

The Wanted

Chasing the Sun

The Wanted

We Own the Night

The Wanted

I Found You

The Weeknd

Blinding Lights

The Weeknd	The White Stripes	The White Stripes
Can't Feel My Face	**Seven Nation Army**	**Fell In Love With a Girl**

The White Stripes	The Who	The Who
The Hardest Button To Button	**Behind Blue Eyes**	**Pinball Wizard**

The Who	The Wonders	Theme Song
Baba O'Riley	**That Thing You Do**	**Duck Tales**

Theme Song	Theme Song	Theme Song
The Aadams Family	**Friends (I'll Be There For You)**	**Pokemon**

Theme Song	They Might Be Giants	Thievery Corporation
The Fresh Prince of Bel-Air	**Experimental Film**	**Lebanese Blonde**

Thin Lizzy	Third Eye Blind	Tim McGraw, Faith Hill
The Boys are Back in Town	**Semi-Charmed Life**	**It's Your Love**

Timbaland, One Republic

Apologize

Tina Turner

What's Love Got To Do With It

Tina Turner

The Best

TLC

Waterfalls

Tom Jones

You're My World

Tones & I

Dance Monkey

Tones & I

Fly Away

Toni Braxton

Unbreak My Heart

Toploader

Dancing In The Moonlight

Toto
Africa

Tracy Chapman
Fast Car

Train
Hey Soul Sister

Train
Drops of Jupiter

twenty one pilots
Stressed Out

twenty one pilots
Ride

twenty one pilots
House Of Gold

twenty one pilots
Chlorine

twenty one pilots
Car Radio

twenty one pilots

Migraine

twenty one pilots

Tear in My Heart

twenty one pilots

Heathens

U2

With Or Without You

U2

I Still Haven't Found
What I'm Looking For

U2

Sunday, Bloody Sunday

UB40

Red Red Wine

Uncle Kracker & Dobie Gray

Drift Away

Usher, Alicia Keys

My Boo

Vance Joy	Vanessa Carlton	Vanilla Ice
Riptide	A Thousand Miles	Ice Ice Baby

Vertical Horizon	Village People	Weezer
Everything You Want	YMCA	Say it Ain't So

Weezer	Weezer	Westlife
Undone (The Sweater Song)	Buddy Holly	If I Let You Go

Wham! Last Christmas 	**Whitney Houston** I Have Nothing 	**Whitney Houston** The Greatest Love Of All 
Whitney Houston Saving All My Love For You 	**Whitney Houston** I Wanna Dance With Somebody 	**Whitney Houston** I Will Always Love You 
Wiz Khalifa ft. Charlie Puth See You Again 	**XXXTENTACION** Changes 	**Zara Larsson** Uncover 

Made in the USA
Las Vegas, NV
19 August 2023

76320114R00085